DIG
DEEPER
into
EXODUS

Andrew Sach & Richard Alldritt

DIG
DEEPER
into
EXODUS

Unearthing OLD TESTAMENT treasure

INTER-VARSITY PRESS
SPCK Group, Studio 101, The Record Hall, 16–16A Baldwin's Gardens, London
EC1N 7RJ, England
Email: ivp@ivpbooks.com
Website: www.ivpbooks.com

© 2010 by Andrew Sach and Richard Alldritt

Andrew Sach and Richard Alldritt have asserted their rights under the Copyright, Designs and Patents Act 1988 to be identified as the Authors of this work.

All rights reserved. No part of this publication may be reproduced, stored in a retrieval system, or transmitted, in any form or by any means, electronic, mechanical, photocopying, recording or otherwise, without the prior permission of the publisher or the Copyright Licensing Agency.

Unless otherwise indicated, Scripture quotations are from The Holy Bible, English Standard Version,® copyright © 2001 by Crossway Bibles, a publishing ministry of Good News Publishers. Used by permission. All rights reserved.

First published 2010 as Dig Even Deeper
Reprinted 2012, 2014
Reissued 2025

British Library Cataloguing in Publication Data
A catalogue record for this book is available from the British Library.

ISBN: 978-1-78974-570-2

Typeset by CRB Associates, Potterhanworth, Lincolnshire
Printed and bound in Great Britain by Ashford Colour Press Ltd, Gosport, Hampshire

Inter-Varsity Press publishes Christian books that are true to the Bible and that communicate the gospel, develop discipleship and strengthen the church for its mission in the world.

Inter-Varsity Press is closely linked with the Universities and Colleges Christian Fellowship, a student movement connecting Christian Unions in universities and colleges throughout Great Britain, and a member movement of the International Fellowship of Evangelical Students. Website: www.uccf.org.uk

Dedication

To Andrew's godson, Thomas Sleeman
and Richard's firstborn, Charlie Alldritt

You may tell in the hearing of your son and of your grandson how I have dealt harshly with the Egyptians and what signs I have done among them, that you may know that I am Yahweh.
(Exodus 10:2)

And when your children say to you, 'What do you mean by this service?' you shall say, 'It is the sacrifice of Yahweh's Passover, for he passed over the houses of the people of Israel in Egypt, when he struck the Egyptians but spared our houses.'
(Exodus 12:26–27)

Contents

Acknowledgments		11
Introduction		13
Beatings	(Exodus 1 – 2)	19
Bush	(Exodus 3:1 – 7:7)	31
Plagues	(Exodus 7:8 – 10:29)	45
Passover	(Exodus 11:1 – 13:16)	55
Water	(Exodus 13:17 – 15:21)	65
Whingeing	(Exodus 15:22 – 17:16)	77
Father-in-law	(Exodus 18)	87
Fear	(Exodus 19:1 – 20:21)	99
Case law	(Exodus 20:22 – 23:33)	113
Covenant	(Exodus 24)	129
Tabernacle	(Exodus 25 – 31)	137
Calf	(Exodus 32:1 – 33:6)	153
Cleft	(Exodus 33:7 – 34:35)	167
Tabernacle	(Exodus 35 – 40)	179
Appendix 1:	Did the Exodus really happen?	187
Appendix 2:	Commentaries, copying and catastrophe!	195
Appendix 3:	The Bible toolkit	199
Notes		203

Acknowledgments

Andrew would like to thank Nigel Beynon (co-author of the original *Dig Deeper*) who first commissioned him to do an overview of Exodus for St Helen's annual student conference, which got the ball rolling for this book. And thanks, Nigel, for your constant friendship and love that are such an encouragement to me.

Richard would like to thank his wife Claire for her endless love, patience and support. And for letting him choose 'Munro' as our son's middle name.

Both of us are grateful to those who taught us God's word, whose love and respect for it were so contagious. Andrew thinks particularly of David Jackman, whose classes on Exodus on the Cornhill Training Course remain influential, and of William Taylor whose desire always, *always* to be guided by the Bible is an enduring example. Richard thinks particularly of Michael You and Leonie Mason who, during the two years of the St Helen's Associate Scheme, helped him understand the Bible more than anyone else.

Thanks to everyone on the Exodus weekends away who learned by heart the twelve-word Exodus summary, and apologies that it's now changed to fourteen entirely different words! Thanks to Sarah Arora, Audrey Brown and Anna Forbes whose cakes fuelled our writing. Thanks to Jonathan Ruffer for his thought-provoking reflections on fearing God. Thanks to Sam Osborne and Ed Shaw for help with proofreading. Thanks to Professor Julian Rivers from Bristol University for his kind response to an email about British law and biblical law. Thanks to Pod Bhogal and all the lovely UCCF staffworkers who said some nice things about a draft of some of the early chapters and helped us to keep going.

Thanks to Eleanor Trotter and the team at IVP for being the best publishers in the world. We love the fact that you don't only publish books well, but that you share with us a love for the God about whom those books speak.

Most of all, of course, we render praise to the God we've both got to know a little better in the pages of Exodus, 'a God merciful and gracious, slow to anger, and abounding in steadfast love and faithfulness, keeping steadfast love for thousands, forgiving iniquity and transgression and sin, but who will by no means clear the guilty . . .' (Exodus 34:6–7).

Andrew Sach
Richard Alldritt
September 2010

With a lighthearted and personal touch, the authors provide an engaging study guide to the book of Exodus. Encouraging contemporary readers to grapple with this extraordinary account of God's rescue of exploited migrant workers, they offer practical advice on how best to discern the ever-relevant message of this important Old Testament book. For anyone keen to discover God's word afresh, here is an excellent starting point.
T. D. Alexander, Senior Lecturer in Biblical Studies, Union Theological College, Belfast

Dig Deeper into Exodus is gold! It's a resource that will introduce even the newest Bible reader to thinking deeply about the message of the Bible. In using a kit of Bible reading tools to the book of Exodus, it demonstrates how a careful handling of the Bible is far more compelling than the shortcuts. I'm looking forward to introducing it to all our Bible study programmes.
Nick Duke, Senior Pastor, Cornerstone Church, Christchurch, New Zealand

For those Christians who find the Old Testament to be a complete and unfathomable mystery (and there are many of them!), here is the book you need to read to get back into the first and major part of God's word! Focusing on the book of Exodus, Andrew and Richard not only unpack the text clearly, but also explain the tools needed to understand the Old Testament and to apply it to twenty-first-century life. This is a great book for everyone wanting to 'dig deep' into the Scriptures in order to see how it speaks to their lives today.
Dr Jamie Grant, Vice Principal, Highland Theological College UHI

Dig Deeper into Exodus takes the 'tools of the Bible-handling trade' out of the toolbox and shows us how to put them to effective use in the book of Exodus. Succinct, accessible, practical and always text-driven, the authors help the Bible teacher plot a straight course through this foundational Bible book. *Dig Deeper into Exodus* is an excellent resource that should be on every church bookstall and in the hand of every small group leader.
Reuben Hunter, Associate Minister, International Presbyterian, Ealing

When I decided to study Exodus with our students this year, I was left scratching my head for a student (not to mention student-worker) friendly resource, until I came across *Dig Deeper into Exodus*. Its genius is that it doesn't just spoon-feed you the 'right' answers, but step by step shows you how – with humility, prayer and a little hard work – you can find the answers for yourself and experience the joy of hearing God speak through this fantastic part of the Bible. The 'student-friendly' style, stretching study questions and numerous worked examples – including some of the authors' false turns to learn from – will give students the tools and the confidence to mine the depths not just of Exodus but the rest of the Bible too. I loved it and can't wait to get it into their hands.
Dr Ben Mandley, Associate Minister, St James, Clerkenwell

Exodus is central to our understanding and experience of salvation, and *Dig Deeper into Exodus* shows us how we can mine the treasure from the book. The writing is engaging and lively, and introduces us to the God of the Exodus with great enthusiasm. Read this book to develop your confidence in handling God's word – but more than that, read this book to be blown away by the God who rescues his people from slavery.
Anna McCracken works for a charity, and is a member of Christ Church, Liverpool

At first glance, you may think this is a curious book: not a commentary, yet containing some great insights into the book of Exodus; not a devotional tool, yet a robust and challenging exposition of the chapters; not a book about technique, yet by applying the Dig Deeper tools it provides a model of how the Bible should be read and understood; not a homiletic manual, yet gold for a preacher or Bible study leader in almost any setting. 'Curiouser and curiouser', as Alice once said. Perhaps – yet here is a wonderfully robust and refreshingly deep analysis of Exodus. It made me want to read Exodus again, study Exodus again, preach Exodus again. And goodness, even I can remember fourteen words!
Adrian Reynolds, Head of National Ministries, Fellowship of Independent Evangelical Churches (FIEC)

Introduction

I (Andrew) have never seen a burning bush, have never suffered a plague of boils (even as a seventeen-year-old the acne wasn't *that* bad), have never parted my bathwater and walked through the middle, have never been to Mount Sinai, let alone heard God speaking from thunder on the top of it, and have never been even remotely tempted to worship an animal made from melted-down earrings. *What possible relevance does the book of Exodus have to me?*

Romans 15:4 is one of the most mind-blowing verses in the whole Bible. More than a thousand years after the events of the Exodus, the apostle Paul was able to say this:

> For whatever was written in former days was written for *our* instruction, that through endurance and through the encouragement of the Scriptures *we* might have hope.
> (Romans 15:4)

Pause to think about that for a moment. Let the implications sink in. God spoke to Moses in the burning bush for our benefit. God visited a plague of boils on Pharaoh for our benefit. God parted the Red Sea for our benefit. God spoke to the people from the mountain for our benefit. Moses recorded the golden-calf episode for our benefit. And we could go on. All the events recorded in the book of Exodus happened for our benefit. It was written for us.

This is a book about what Exodus means for us today. We're going to go through all forty chapters, retelling the story, puzzling over some of the details and discerning what God has to say to us. For us as authors, it's meant every Friday morning for over a year, thumbing the pages of the Bible, discovering many things we've never seen before, glimpsing something of the glory of the God who calls himself 'I AM' (Exodus 3:14). We've had a *lot* of fun writing this, and we hope that some of our enthusiasm will rub off on you too.

Dig deeper

But it's not our aim simply to tell you what Exodus means. We want to share with you *why* we think it means what it does, how we came to this understanding, and what discoveries we made. Rather than a Hollywood movie, this book is going to be more like the 'how-they-made-the-movie' footage that you get on the DVD extras.

We set about discovering the message of Exodus using various tools. The **Repetition tool** helped us to see that God's name is a big deal, in chapter 6. The **Context tool** showed us why it was important to beat the Amalekites, in chapter 17. The **Quotation/Allusion tool** uncovered a miniature garden of Eden where we least expected one. And so on. The Bible toolkit was first introduced in *Dig Deeper*, another little book published by IVP. In *Dig Deeper into Exodus* the toolkit goes 'live'. We're going to try to show you how to get to grips with a whole Bible book from beginning to end.

We're passionate that Christians should learn the tools of the Bible-handling trade, because of what the apostle Paul wrote to Timothy (the theme verse of the original *Dig Deeper* too):

> Do your best to present yourself to God as one approved, a worker who has no need to be ashamed, rightly handling the word of truth. (2 Timothy 2:15)

A few years ago Andrew lived in Peckham, South London, in a house with bad plumbing. The kitchen tap dripped all the time – we had to take out gym membership to develop the muscles necessary to turn it fully off. And a faulty ball valve in the upstairs loo meant that water poured continually out of the overflow pipe, giving the neighbours' garden a not-so-attractive water feature. Our water bills were becoming expensive. Cue Ray, the local plumber we found in Yellow Pages. He couldn't do anything about the kitchen tap, but he did manage to stop the loo overflowing . . . and flushing! In short, Ray turned out to be a cowboy plumber.

Join Andrew for his recurring nightmare. He's in hospital, about to undergo heart surgery. Just before the anaesthetic kicks in, he catches a glimpse of the face of the surgeon who is set to perform the operation. It's Ray, smiling, wielding a scalpel with the same deftness with which he handled the monkey wrench. Noooooo!

Cowboy plumbers are one thing, but cowboy surgeons are quite another.

So is handling the Bible more like changing the washer on a tap or changing a heart valve? If you get it wrong, are people going to have toilets that don't flush or will they die? Actually explaining the Bible is *infinitely* more significant even than heart surgery, because if you get it right people will live for *ever*. But if you get it wrong . . .

History is littered with cowboy theologians, cowboy preachers, cowboy Sunday school teachers. In the recent history of South Africa, for example, a twisted reading of Exodus 19:6 was used as a justification for the despicable practice of apartheid; Exodus was also mishandled by some of the liberation theologians, who made the gospel only about deliverance from political oppression ('let my people go') and discarded all notions of salvation from sin and God's judgment.

It matters that you get the Bible right. We pray that God will use this little book to that end.

Getting the most out of this book
Dig Deeper into Exodus is designed to be an interactive experience, but the level of interactivity is partly down to you. There are exercises in most chapters so you can practise using the tools for yourself, and a number of 'Brainbox Asides' for those who want to be stretched even further.

Now we need to ask you a favour. Please don't turn the page until you have read the whole of Exodus from cover to cover. What? Surely we are not serious? Yes, we really mean it. After all, *Dig Deeper into Exodus* was written on a Macbook by a couple of blokes in East London; the book of Exodus was breathed out by the Holy Spirit. It would be a tragedy if you read less of the Bible than you read of our comments! Read Exodus fairly quickly. Don't get bogged down in the detail. Look out for the big themes. Start to get a feel for what's going on.

Read Exodus before turning over!

Hello again. How was that? First impressions? It's pretty rip-roaring stuff, isn't it? You probably noticed eleven plagues (the one you might have missed comes in chapter 32), a fair bit of whingeing about food, a lot of God wanting people to 'know that I am the Lord', Moses' apparent fondness for hiking up mountains, and a pretty remarkable sea crossing. Quite a lot to take in.

We had a go boiling it all down to a fourteen-word summary (at least it's fourteen if you allow us to cheat a bit with hyphens). You can probably do better. But we came up with this:

Beatings
Bush
Plagues
Passover
Water
Whingeing
Father-in-law
Fear
Case law
Covenant
Tabernacle
Calf
Cleft
Tabernacle

Off we go . . .

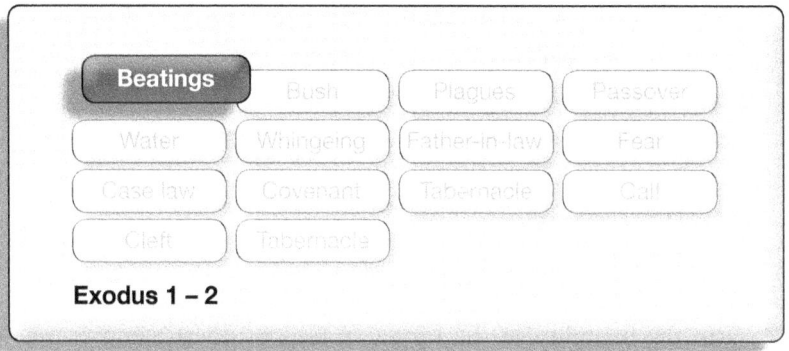

Exodus 1 – 2

Does God have amnesia?
In April 1975 the Khmer Rouge seized power in Cambodia. During their four-year reign of terror it is estimated that somewhere between 1.4 and 2 million Cambodians died from disease, starvation or torture. Pol Pot systematically executed anyone he felt might pose a threat to his regime. His paranoia extended to anyone with an education – simply wearing glasses marked you out as a potential target for the death squads. Many teachers were killed, many doctors, many Christians.

This leaves people asking why. Why does God allow people, especially his people, to suffer in this way? Is he too weak to stop it? Does he even care? Those are the kind of questions that God's people would have been asking in Exodus 1 – 2.

Even though the book of Genesis had a happy ending (Joseph is mates with the king of Egypt and negotiates shelter for the twelve tribes of Israel during a severe famine), it only takes a few verses at the start of Exodus for things to turn sour. Joseph dies; there's a change of government; and there's a dramatic shift in immigration policy. Overnight Goshen, the area housing the Israelite refugees, turns into a labour camp.

> Therefore they set taskmasters over them to afflict them with heavy burdens. They built for Pharaoh store cities, Pithom and Raamses . . . So they ruthlessly made the people of Israel work as slaves and made their lives bitter with hard service, in mortar and brick, and in all kinds of work in the field. In all their work they ruthlessly made them work as slaves.
> (1:11, 13–14)

But the brutality of the Egyptian regime doesn't end there. An official memo arrives at the maternity ward of Goshen General Hospital ordering the termination of all male Israelite children. By the end of the chapter, the whole population is instructed to drown Israelite boys in the river. Today we call it ethnic cleansing. It's Auschwitz and Belsen in the 1940s; Cambodia in the 1970s; Yugoslavia and Rwanda in the 1990s; the Democratic Republic of Congo as we write. A humanitarian disaster with an absent God in a remote heaven who does nothing. Or so it seems.

And so the end of chapter 2 comes as a bit of a relief:

> During those many days the king of Egypt died, and the people of Israel groaned because of their slavery and cried out for help. Their cry for rescue from slavery came up to God. And God heard their groaning, and God remembered his covenant with Abraham, with Isaac, and with Jacob.
> (2:23–24)

God has been suffering two chapters of amnesia, but a king's funeral triggers his memory. Finally he wakes up and is about to do something.

But that can't be right, can it?

An interpretation of the Bible that makes God look like someone with amnesia? It can't be right. We must have got the wrong end of the stick somehow. There must be more going on. You're reading this book because you want to 'dig deeper', and you're probably eager to get your hands dirty with some Bible tools. If ever there was a need to look more closely at a passage, this is it.

Using the **Structure tool**, we noticed that Jacob pops up at the beginning and the end of our section. The book opens in 1:1 with a reference to 'the sons of Israel who came . . . with Jacob' (he actually gets mentioned twice here, because 'Israel' and 'Jacob' are two names for the same person). And the section closes in 2:24 with a reference to the 'covenant with Abraham, with Isaac, and with Jacob'. We realized that, like a pair of bookends, these two allusions to Jacob's family tree enclose the whole section.

Jacob's family is so important in the Old Testament that the writer assumes we will see the significance immediately. If you don't, and the secret is still hidden from you, then it may be time for the next tool:

Quotation/Allusion tool

Read Genesis 12:1–2, 7. What does God promise Abraham?

Read Genesis 26:3–4. What does God promise Isaac (Abraham's son)?

Read Genesis 28:3–4. What does God promise Jacob (Abraham's grandson)?

So when the author of Exodus says that God 'remembered his covenant with Abraham, with Isaac, and with Jacob', what kind of things is he intending to bring to mind?

God and Pharaoh step into the ring

Once you've done the background work in Genesis you'll start seeing the holes in the amnesia theory. It seems that 2:24 isn't so much a statement of the next thing that happened in chronological sequence (the king died . . . *then* God remembered) as a summary of the whole of the action so far. In a subtle, behind-the-scenes way, God *has been remembering* his promises to Jacob's family all along.

We've made it a rule that we're not allowed to tell you the answers to the Dig Deeper exercises, but you'll forgive us if we break it just this once. Hopefully you saw something in Genesis about God wanting Jacob to have a big family – 'be fruitful and multiply', 'as numerous as the stars in the sky' – that kind of thing. God wants the population to go up. Pharaoh on the other hand is wary of the military threat posed by Israel's increasing numbers (1:9–10). He wants the population to go down. Read from the start of chapter 1 again, with this in mind, and you will see things a little differently.

God and Pharaoh step into the ring. The bell goes. Round 1.

God gets off to a strong start in verse 7. Before you know it Israel is fruitful and multiplying. But Pharaoh is quick out of the red corner and announces his first counter-blow. Oppress the Israelites with forced labour! When they finally get home to their wives they'll think of nothing but sleep!

Pharaoh's wild swing missed the mark. The taskmasters increase the workload, but unexpectedly it only increases the activity between the sheets: 'the more they were oppressed, the more they multiplied and the more they spread' (1:12). The bell sounds the end of Round 1, and the king of Egypt is already nursing a cut lip.

Round 2 begins and Pharaoh decides to play dirty with the help of (OK, so this stretches our boxing metaphor a bit) some midwives. Fortunately these women fear the LORD (verse 17) more than they fear Pharaoh and refuse to kill the baby boys. When interviewed later, they get away with an excuse *so bad* that you know God must be involved:

> Hebrew women are not like the Egyptian women, for they are vigorous and give birth before the midwife comes to them.
> (1:19)

If you're confused about why the midwives receive God's approval for telling such a blatant porky when the Bible generally commends truthfulness, we'd really recommend the discussion by John Frame in 📖 *The Doctrine of the Christian Life*.[1] The author of Exodus doesn't dwell on these thorny ethical issues; his point is simply that the population continues to climb. At the end of Round 2 Pharaoh is sitting in his corner, looking decidedly punch-drunk.

Round 3 opens with Pharaoh out of control, fists flying in all directions. 'Drown every Israelite boy,' he cries (verse 22). This time, instead of telling us about the population as a whole, the narrator zooms in to explain how one particular family dodges the blow . . .

It's hard to imagine what it must be like to raise a child in the knowledge that an execution squad is prowling the streets looking for him. He wakes during the night, and you hurry to muffle his cries. You bury the nappies in the garden in case the secret police are going through the rubbish. We're told this particular mum kept her baby hidden for three months; it must have seemed like years. Eventually she runs out of options and hides him among the reeds by the river bank. Pharaoh had ordered that the babies be thrown in the Nile, and she can manage little better – the only difference is a little papyrus basket (2:3).[2]

This is the time to get out the **Translations tool**. If you have a KJV or NKJV Bible to hand, or you look at the footnote in the TNIV (all of these translations and more are available online at www.biblegateway.com), you will find that the papyrus basket is called an 'ark'. That sounds familiar of course, and before long we're using the **Quotation/Allusion tool** again to see if this has got anything to do with Noah's famous boat. We dutifully re-check the Noah account, and there we discover that his ark had to be waterproofed with pitch (Genesis 6:14), a procedure very similar to that used to waterproof the floating cot here in Exodus.

I (Andrew) ought to come clean and admit that I only spotted this because we had to learn the Hebrew word for 'ark' at Bible college. At the time I was a bit put out: learning the word for a rare type of boat mentioned in only two Bible stories seemed to take our vocabulary learning to unnecessary extremes. I'm now chuffed of course, because in God's providence it's helping me write a book on Exodus years later! It's always a good idea to check multiple translations because occasionally you'll pick up something cool like this for yourself.

The baby Israelite is saved through an ark, of all things. Why? Presumably because the God who's at work behind the scenes wants us to discern his hand in it. You might say that salvation-by-ark is something of a signature move! Even as Pharaoh tries to drown babies, God saves them. At the close of Round 3 it looks as if Pharaoh's close to throwing in the towel.

Round 4 is the slapstick round. It's not so much boxing as WWE. Pharaoh's daughter discovers a cute Hebrew baby among the reeds, but her broody-hen tendencies are in conflict with her princess tendencies – princesses don't change nappies! As luck would have it, a passing Israelite girl (strategically positioned elder sister) has the phone number of an excellent nanny (strategically positioned mother) to whom the princess offers a generous financial package. So let's just summarize: the baby that Pharaoh wanted to kill is now being raised by Moses' own mother at the expense of Pharaoh's daughter. God really is taking the mick.

Did you notice that we don't find out the name on the birth certificate until right at the end? It's Moses. But before we get into the sea-parting, stone-tablet-carrying activities for which he is later famous, his childhood teaches us that God is faithful. Behind the scenes God keeps his promises to Abraham, to Isaac and to Jacob. Pharaoh (not for the last time) is confounded.

Does Moses really stuff things up?
If promise-keeping is the big theme, the next episode comes as a bit of a shock. It doesn't seem to fit. Everything that was going so well seems to go so wrong.

I mean, you can guess God's plan can't you? A Hebrew baby raised in the royal household. As he grows up, it would have been Pharaoh pushing the buggy around the Pyramids. You can imagine Moses as an eight- or nine-year-old sitting on Pharaoh's knee asking his 'granddad' why people had to be so mean to the slaves. You can imagine Pharaoh's heart softening. You can smell a diplomatic solution just around the corner.

So why oh why does Moses have to stuff it all up?

> One day, when Moses had grown up, he went out to his people and looked on their burdens, and he saw an Egyptian beating a Hebrew,

one of his people. He looked this way and that, and seeing no one, he struck down the Egyptian and hid him in the sand.
(2:11–12)

Yes, well done Moses. Nice one. So now the Israelites don't trust you (2:14), and Pharaoh wants to kill you (2:15), and you have to run away to Midian, some 200 miles away. How exactly are you planning to rescue the Israelites from there?!

So God has a plan, but even he can't foolproof it against the actions of a muppet like Moses. And so God ends up frustrated, sitting in heaven saying 'bother', shaking his head and going back to the drawing board to try to think up Plan B.

But that can't be right, can it? An interpretation of the Bible in which God's plans look as precarious as a Jenga tower in the advanced stages of the game? It can't be right.

Apart from theological common sense, the other thing that showed us we'd got the wrong end of the stick was the **Quotation/Allusion tool**. This is useful not only when the Exodus passage alludes back to something earlier in the Bible (as with the Abraham, Isaac and Jacob example), but also when a later Bible writer alludes back to Exodus. In this case there are two relevant New Testament texts: Acts 7:23–29, 35 and Hebrews 11:24–26. Neither attaches any blame to Moses. Stephen (in Acts) points the finger at the Israelites for failing to trust Moses' leadership, while the writer of Hebrews tells us that Moses was acting 'by faith' when he chose to identify himself with the Israelite oppressed.

And so the **Quotation/Allusion tool** sends us back into the Exodus text, armed with the perspective that Moses is acting *faithfully*. To be honest, we puzzled over this. We couldn't see it at first. Even with all the tools, understanding the Bible isn't always easy, and you have to pray and ponder and pray. In the end the solution we found most satisfying came from a commentary: Moses' seemingly crazy actions in chapter 2 are actually a sneak preview of what God is about to do through him in chapters 3 – 15. If you look closely you can see the rescue plan in miniature.

(Commentaries are worth their weight in gold when you get into a tight spot, but they can also lead you badly astray. Check out the appendix on 'Commentaries, copying and catastrophe!' for a few health warnings.)

Actions of Moses	Actions of God
One day, when Moses had grown up . . . he *saw* an Egyptian beating a Hebrew, one of his people (2:11).	Then the LORD said, 'I have surely *seen* the affliction of my people who are in Egypt' (3:7). 'I have also *seen* the oppression with which the Egyptians oppress them' (3:9).
He *struck down* the Egyptian and hid him in the sand (2:12).	'I will pass through the land of Egypt that night, and I will *strike* all the firstborn in the land of Egypt, both man and beast' (12:12). At midnight the LORD *struck down* all the firstborn in the land of Egypt (12:29).
The shepherds came and drove them away, but Moses stood up and *saved* them, and watered their flock (2:17).	Thus the LORD *saved* Israel that day from the hand of the Egyptians (14:30).

Actions of Moses	Actions of God
They said, 'An Egyptian *delivered* us out of the hand of the shepherds' (2:19).	'I have come down to *deliver* them out of the hand of the Egyptians' (3:8).
	Jethro said, 'Blessed be the LORD, who has *delivered* you out of the hand of the Egyptians and out of the hand of Pharaoh and has *delivered* the people from under the hand of the Egyptians' (18:10).

We need to take care how we apply this. Obviously Exodus is not giving us carte blanche to strike down anyone we feel is oppressing a fellow Christian (so your friend at church gets a hard time in the office from her colleagues and you turn up the next day with a baseball bat . . .). There is something unique about the way Moses acts as God's agent. Somehow his striking is God's striking; his delivering is God's delivering. (Much more of this in the coming chapters.)

The battle to trust that God is in control
As we've dug deeper into Exodus 1 – 2, our initial impressions of an absent God in a remote heaven have been blown out of the water. God never abandoned his people, never turned a blind eye to their suffering, never forgot his promises. Yet much of God's activity in these chapters was behind the scenes, discernible only with the benefit of hindsight. Few of his secret victories would have been visible to an Israelite family at the time. It's not until the ark-floated, princess-adopted baby is *eighty* (Acts 7:23, 30) that the rescue plan goes public. It was a long wait.

Exodus 1 – 2 is telling us to trust that God is faithful even when you can't see what he's up to. He hasn't promised health and wealth for everyone who has 'enough faith', as some teach. He hasn't promised freedom from persecution – if anything, the opposite (Acts 14:22; 1 Thessalonians 3:3–4). He *has* promised, however, in fulfilment of his covenant with Abraham, Isaac and Jacob, to multiply his people and to bring them safely to the Promised Land of the new heavens and new earth.

Perhaps recession hits your business. You never thought that you'd end up reading John's Gospel with ten unbelievers at work in the time freed up by cancelled client meetings. The leader of your church at university is diagnosed with gallbladder cancer. You don't anticipate that hundreds of Christians will be strengthened by his steadfast confidence in the resurrection to come. Your teenage son leaves home in Zimbabwe in search of work in Cape Town, swims a crocodile-infested river and jumps from a second-storey window to escape from imprisonment as an illegal immigrant, only to fall victim to xenophobic attacks soon after arrival (true story). You don't guess that God plans to re-house the Zimbabwean immigrants temporarily in the buildings of Christchurch, Somerset West, where your son will hear the gospel and be saved. These are the real-life stories of people we know, people with an Exodus 1 – 2 testimony. Perhaps you have one too.

In his book *Killing Fields, Living Fields*,[3] Don Cormack recounts the story of the church in Cambodia under Pol Pot. He tells of the appalling injustices, the Christian families who were slaughtered. And he tells of the faithfulness of God behind the scenes, how he kept his people, how he grew his kingdom.

Behind-the-scenes faithfulness is God's style. We find it again and again in the pages of Scripture. Even Jesus has an Exodus 1 – 2 testimony. We thought that a fitting place to end.

Quotation/Allusion tool

Read the account of Jesus' infancy in Matthew 2.

Can you find any similarities with Moses' childhood?

- Any Pharaoh-like tyranny? Any 'why-does-God-allow-such-suffering' moments?

- Any signs of God's faithfulness behind the scenes?

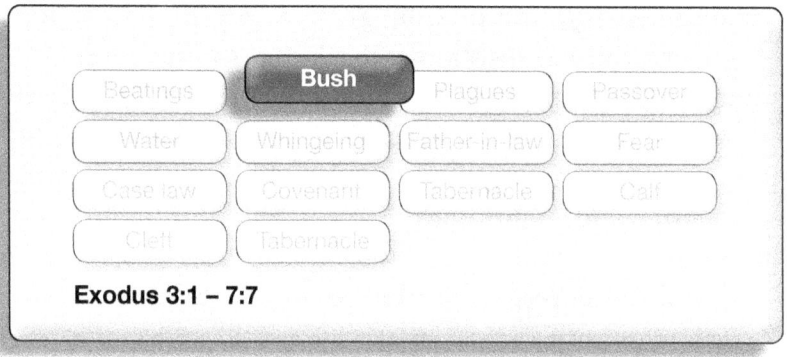

Exodus 3:1 – 7:7

I (Richard) recently became a father, and so for a while baby names were a hot topic of conversation. (We eventually settled on 'Charlie'.) Some people argue that the name you choose can have an enormous impact on the future of your child. There may well be an element of truth in this. After all, when Mr and Mrs Presley called their son Elvis, he was always going to grow up to be a rock 'n' roll singer. Sometimes a name can tell you a lot about a person: where they come from (someone called Hamish McDougall probably isn't from Birmingham), how old they are (not many babies named Adolf after 1945!), what they do (there's a good bet that Snoop Dogg isn't a ballet dancer).

This chapter is about God's name. What he calls himself, and what that means.

The Yahweh name mug

So basically, chapter 3 goes a bit like this: Moses is minding his own business, working as a shepherd for Zippy's dad, when he's interrupted by a fireball. It turns out that God is using a bush as a public address system, announcing his plans to rescue his people. Moses, hurriedly removing his sandals, is understandably scared. God graciously allows time for questions, and we expect Moses to take the opportunity to find out how God flameproofed the bush, or (more sensibly) exactly how God plans to defeat Pharaoh. Instead, he asks probably the most important question in the whole of the book of Exodus:

> If I come to the people of Israel and say to them, 'The God of your fathers has sent me to you', and they ask me, 'What is his name?' what shall I say to them?
> (3:13)

The **Context tool** helps us to understand a bit more of the significance of Moses' questions. So far in the book, names have had meanings. 'Moses' means 'fished out', as a perpetual memory of his rescue from the Nile as a baby (2:10). 'Gershom' means 'asylum seeker', in commemoration of his dad's immigration status at the time (2:22). The name sums up the person, or tells you something fundamental about them.

So when Moses asks God his name, he's really asking 'Who are you? Tell me who I'm dealing with?' God's answer is 'I AM WHO I AM' (3:14). It's a denial of comparisons with other things, a refusal to be slotted into any pre-existing categories. 'Sorry for a bit of a mind-bending answer Moses,' God seems to say, 'but the fact is, I can't tell you what I'm "like" because I'm not like anything or anyone else. The only person in the universe that comes even close to me is . . . me.'

Time for a little aside here. When we get to chapter 6, we'll see that God's name seems to change from 'I AM' to 'LORD':

> I appeared to Abraham, to Isaac, and to Jacob, as God Almighty, but by my name *the* Lord I did not make myself known to them.
> (6:3)

Even more confusingly, in our routine use of the **Translations tool** we found another couple of possibilities:

> I appeared to Abraham, to Isaac, and to Jacob as El-Shaddai – 'God Almighty' – but I did not reveal my name, *Yahweh*, to them.
> (6:3, NLT)

> And I appeared unto Abraham, unto Isaac, and unto Jacob, by the name of God Almighty; but by my name *Jehovah* was I not known to them.
> (6:3, KJV)

So what is God's name? Is it I am or Lord or Yahweh or Jehovah?! If you'll forgive us for going into schoolteacher mode, we thought it was probably time to get out some chalk and find a blackboard:

- In the original Hebrew, the name given in 6:3 is spelt with just four consonants, YHWH.
- The letters YHWH derive from the Hebrew for 'I am'. It's just a shorthand version of the name given at the burning bush.
- Because you can't write YHWH in Greek letters, the New Testament writers (who wrote in Greek) used the word for 'Lord' instead.
- Most English Bibles follow this lead, and translate YHWH using 'Lord' in capitals.

- Other English Bibles decide to stick to YHWH, but add some vowels to make it more pronounceable. For historic reasons, which we won't go into, they used to add e-o-a to give YeHoWaH = Jehovah. Nowadays they simply add a-e to give Yahweh.

When it comes to the book of Exodus, we prefer the translation 'Yahweh' over 'Lord', because it sounds less like a title and more like a *name*. It reminds us that we're getting to know someone personally. So from now on we're going to use Yahweh whenever we quote from the Bible.

So far so good. But we still haven't got that far in working out what Yahweh *means*. You know those tacky name mugs that you get in motorway service stations that tell you that 'Andrew' means 'manly' and 'Richard' means 'powerful leader' (for example)? Well what would go on a 'Yahweh' name mug? What does the name stand for?

In 3:15, we learn that Yahweh is none other than 'the God of your fathers, the God of Abraham, the God of Isaac, and the God of Jacob' (3:15). That should make you sit up in your seat.

Context tool

What is significant about the mention of Abraham, Isaac and Jacob?

Is there anything else in Exodus 3 that is reminiscent of the Abraham, Isaac and Jacob context? Which of the promises in Genesis does God repeat here?

How would this revelation of God's name provide Moses with much-needed encouragement, given his current circumstances?

Picking up the narrative in Exodus 5, Moses turns up in Pharaoh's court with a request:

'Please can we go and worship God?'
'Not on your nelly.'

Negotiations are not entirely successful, to say the least. As in chapter 1, we are given an appalling glimpse of the conditions in the concentration camp. Yahweh's brief appearance in a bush hasn't made a lot of difference so far. If anything, things have got worse.

The **Tone and Feel tool** reminds us to pay attention not just to the point being made, but also to how it is being made. If all you wanted to do was report the facts, you could boil chapter 5 down to six words: 'Same brick quota; straw not provided.' But the author is doing more than reporting facts. He wants to capture the sense of injustice, the sheer brutality of Pharaoh's regime.

Notice

- The unreasonable demand: 'Go and get your straw yourselves wherever you can find it, but your work will not be reduced in the least' (verse 11).
- The ongoing cries of the taskmasters: 'Complete your work, your daily task each day, as when there was straw' (verse 13).
- The perverse questions: 'Why have you not done all your task of making bricks today and yesterday, as in the past?' (verse 14).
- The desperation of the Israelite foremen: 'Why do you treat your servants like this? No straw is given to your servants, yet they say to us, "Make bricks!"' (verses 15b–16a).

- Pharaoh's shocking dismissal of their complaint: 'You are idle, you are idle' (verse 17).

How are you feeling? Is your blood starting to boil? It should be. The author draws us into the story so that we *feel* how desperately, desperately wrong it all is. But buried within chapter 5 is the key to exactly what is wrong. We might miss it if it were not for the **Context tool**. We know that the surrounding chapters are all about God's name, and so our ears can't help but prick up when we hear Pharaoh's words (his first recorded words in the book of Exodus):

> Who is Yahweh, that I should obey his voice and let Israel go? I do not know Yahweh, and moreover, I will not let Israel go.
> (5:2)

Behind Pharaoh's brutality lies an ignorance of the one whom he's dealing with. The name Yahweh means nothing to him.

Ironically, Moses and the Israelites have the same problem. They ought to know better, because of what happened at the bush, but notice the wording of Moses' complaint:

> Then Moses turned to Yahweh and said, 'O Lord, why have you done evil to this people? Why did you ever send me? For since I came to Pharaoh to speak *in your name*, he has done evil to this people, and you have not delivered your people at all.'
> (5:22–23)

As chapter 5 draws to a close, the issue is brand recognition. YAHWEH. It means nothing to God's enemies. It means little more to God's people. We need Yahweh to explain himself once again, and that's exactly what he does at the start of chapter 6.

It's a bit repetitive, which gives us the perfect excuse to try out the **Repetition tool**.

Repetition tool

Read 6:1–11. Then re-read the original revelation of God's name back in 3:1–22.

What repeated phrases can you find?

What aspects of God's character is he keen to emphasize?

Can you summarize this in a few words that would be appropriate for the side of a Yahweh name mug?

Before we move on, we wanted to pick out a phrase from chapter 6 that's going to become very important in the rest of the book:

You shall know that I am Yahweh your God.
(6:7)

Notice it doesn't say that you know *now*. Sure, he has explained himself. But that doesn't mean we get it. It's the difference between understanding something in theory and believing it in practice. We'll only really understand God's name when we spend time with him, listen to him, watch him in action. That's what the rest of the book of Exodus is for.

Why not stop and pray now? Ask God that as you read on he would reveal himself to you, that you would learn about his name and his character.

Moses, the coward

You may have noticed that we're tackling this chapter in a bit of a strange order. If you didn't notice, then you're trusting us too much. 'Why did they miss out chapter 4?' you should be asking yourself. 'Is this Ray-the-plumber Bible handling?'

Just to reassure you, we have no intention of skipping chapter 4. We've done it this way because when we first came to this passage we used the **Structure tool**. That's almost always the best way to start, especially when you're dealing with a whopping four chapters in one go.

When we used the **Structure tool** we found a repeating pattern. It begins with a revelation of God's name (3:1–22; 6:1–11), followed by a description of Moses as a bit of a coward (4:1–31; 6:12–30). The first time round it ends in failure, with Moses rejected by Pharaoh and Israel (5:1–23). The second time God promises success.

    A. God's name (3:1–22)
       B. Moses is a coward (4:1–31)
          C. Moses' mission fails (5:1–23)
    A. God's name (6:1–11)
       B. Moses is a coward (6:12–30)
          C. God promises success (7:1–7)

Once we noticed this structure we thought we'd tackle the two 'A' sections together – the bits about God's name – before going on to look at the 'B' bits about Moses. But now it's time for the 'B' bits.

One popular approach to the material about Moses in 4:1–31 is to turn it into a church leadership manual. Perhaps this is what creates the market for the '59-inch hickory Moses hiking staff' that you can buy from amazon.com – no kidding. We got a bit nervous about that approach when we started using the **'Who am I?' tool**, and tried to work out which of the characters in the book (if any) the author intends us to identify with. The safe bet is to put ourselves in the shoes of an ordinary Israelite. After all they are God's people, rescued out of slavery in order that they might worship him. There are lots of Israelites, just as there are lots of Christians. There is only one Moses. But strangely we all want to be him.

We discussed the Moses-is-me syndrome in the original *Dig Deeper*. It refers to our propensity to identify ourselves with the hero of any story. If we're not careful we can end up asking silly questions like 'what burning-bush experiences have *you* had?', the answer of course being none, apart from that unfortunate incident with the firework and the neighbours' pampas grass. To read Exodus 3 and assume that we must have had our own individual burning-bush experiences is like reading Genesis 1 and assuming that we have had individual creating-the-world experiences! Moses is not me, and many of the things that he does as leader and rescuer of God's people foreshadow the life of Christ much more than the lives of everyday Christians. Having said that, *sometimes* Moses is held up as a model believer (e.g. Hebrews 11:24–29). It might sometimes be right to ask **'Who am I?'** and step into Moses' shoes. To read of Moses' cowardice and reflect on our own failure to trust God, or our church leaders' failure to trust God, may not be completely wide of the mark.

However, the author has a different purpose in mind for the two 'B' sections. Moses is about to do some pretty amazing stuff. His staff turns into a snake at will (don't think this is a feature of the Amazon.com version!). He leads the people through the Red Sea on dry ground. The Israelites win a battle just because he holds his hands in the air. Quite an impressive

CV. But before Moses does any of this, the writer wants us to be clear that he would be nothing without the empowering grace of Yahweh.

You know that you're on track with the **Author's Purpose tool** when lots of different bits of the chapter point in the same direction. Again and again the writer makes clear that the hero is Yahweh, not Moses. We see it first in the extended dialogue that runs from 3:11 to 4:17. To paraphrase it slightly . . .

> Moses says: 'But I'm not up to the job' (3:11).
> Yahweh says: 'That's irrelevant Moses. The only thing that counts is that I'll be with you' (3:12).
>
> Moses says: 'But who are you?' (3:13).
> Yahweh says: 'Don't worry Moses, my name is Yahweh. This is what my name means . . .' (3:14).
>
> Moses says: 'But they'll never believe me' (4:1).
> Yahweh says: 'That's why I'm giving you some James Bond-style tricks – they'll believe you when you perform these before the people' (4:2–9).
>
> Moses says: 'But I'm not much of a public speaker' (4:10).
> Yahweh says: 'I made your mouth and I'll tell you what to say' (4:11–12).
>
> Moses says: 'But please send someone else' (4:13).
> Yahweh says: 'Take your elder brother with you' (4:14–16).

You don't come out of that still thinking of Moses as a leadership guru. He is a coward. But Yahweh is full of grace and can achieve his purposes, even through an old frightened shepherd who's spent the last forty years living in the backwater of Midian.

Moses' dependence on Yahweh is emphasized for a second time when we come to 4:24–26. This is one of those twists in the story that persuades your adrenal gland to spice up your bloodstream! Just when you thought that everything was going well, 'Yahweh met him and sought to put him to death.'

What?!

Fasten your seat belts; this bit is tricky! To start with, we need to give you a preview of chapter 12 (sort of like using the **Context tool** backwards): the firstborn sons of the Israelites will be saved from God's judgment by means of the death of a lamb whose blood is smeared on the doorframes of their houses. Hopefully you can see how this is foreshadowed here in chapter 4. There is a mention of firstborn sons in verses 22–23. And someone's life is spared through blood in verses 25–26. It's not actually clear in the original whether it's Moses' life that was on the line or that of his firstborn son: the Hebrew just says that Yahweh was about to kill 'him' in verse 24, and in verses 25–26 the 'bridegroom' word just means 'family member', so Zippy could be talking about either her husband or her son. When the Bible is ambiguous like this, it's best to think of it as being *deliberately* ambiguous. Presumably the Holy Spirit, as he inspired the writer, intended us to associate Moses' fate with the fate of firstborn sons. So in a book where firstborn sons are to be rescued by blood sacrifice, Moses gets rescued in the same way. Are you still with us?

The point is this: Moses the saviour needs saving himself. In fact, this is the second time Moses has been rescued in just four chapters – remember the ark? Some writers point out that both times it's a woman who saves the day: first Moses' sister, and then his wife. But while these women of God are very cool, they are not ultimately the heroes. Yahweh is the hero. That's the author's purpose.

The same point is made again in the second 'B' section, 6:12–30. Check out the emphasis using the **Repetition tool**:

> But Moses said to Yahweh, 'Behold the people of Israel have not listened to me. How then shall Pharaoh listen to me, for I am of uncircumcised lips?'
> (6:12)

And again:

> But Moses said to Yahweh, 'Behold, I am of uncircumcised lips. How will Pharaoh listen to me?'
> (6:30)

We get the point. Moses is scared silly. And notice where this comes in the overall structure – *after* God has revealed his name a second time. Moses is supposed to be reassured by now, but he's still shaking like a leaf. Yahweh is the only one who has any confidence in Pharaoh's downfall, and the glory will be his alone.

So What? tool

You should be asking 'so what?' at the end of every Bible passage you ever read. After all, God wants to change us, not just fill our heads with words.

Read 2 Corinthians 12:9.

Reflect on how this principle is seen in the 'B' sections above.

If we think of Moses as a 'hero' in his own right, how might we subtly diminish God's grace?

To what other human heroes are you personally tempted to give a share of God's glory? Who gets the credit for the successful ministry in your church, for example?

How does God's decision to work through a weak and cowardly Moses encourage you?

BRAINBOX ASIDE: Genealogy

Before all the plague action kicks off, the author decided to press 'pause', interrupt the narrative and give us a genealogy for Moses and Aaron (6:14–25). Perhaps the idea is simply to root Moses and Aaron in the history books, to convince us that this really happened. But in that case . . .

Why

- does the genealogy come in between a pair of 'uncircumcised-lips' bookends (verses 12, 30)?
- do we get so much detail about the Levite tribe (compared with other branches of the family tree that are omitted), and why do we hear about Aaron's descendants and not those of Moses? It could be something to do with the priesthood: Levi was the priestly tribe; Aaron was chief priest; and God makes a 'covenant of a lasting priesthood' with Phinehas in the book of Numbers (25:10–13). But if so, why focus on the priesthood *here*?

Happy digging!

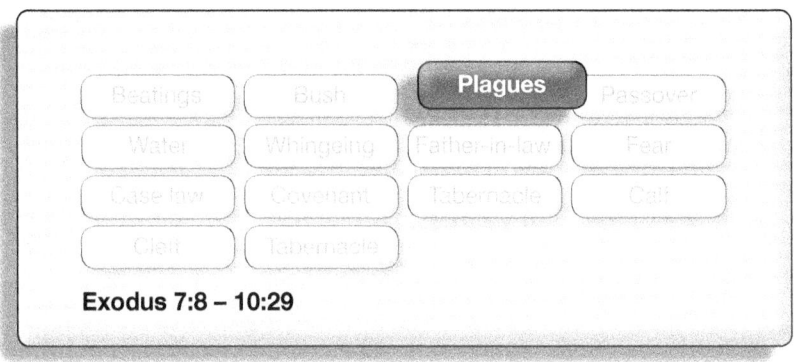

Exodus 7:8 – 10:29

Richard is a 'Munro Bagger', which means he's aiming to climb all of the Scottish mountains over 3,000 feet. At the time of writing it's 188 down, 95 to go. Thought bubble from Andrew: 'Why would you voluntarily put yourself through an experience that so closely resembles Egypt under the plagues? This is insanity.'

Take the Scottish weather for example (apologies to Scottish readers). While hailstones large enough to slay cattle will make an Englishman's eyes pop out, they barely raise an eyebrow north of the border. In winter it gets dark so early in Inverness that a plague of darkness could go unnoticed for weeks. But undoubtedly the most Scottish of all the plagues is number 3. The Highland midge may be tiny, but pound for pound it devours more human flesh than a piranha. Andrew was once so foolish as to attend an open-air performance of *Romeo and Juliet* on the West coast of Scotland in August. By the time Romeo drank the poison, we were too busy scratching even to feel sad. You have to pity Richard's friend, who had a summer job testing the relative effectiveness of different insect repellents as she sat at the side of the loch, both arms bared. Genuinely.

The thing is, the events of Exodus 7 – 10 aren't as 'comedy' as jokes about Scotland. Blood coming out of the kitchen tap doesn't get a lot of laughs. Neither does the famine that follows a locust swarm. God doesn't send the plagues to raise a smile.

Why were there ten plagues?

Remember that the **Author's Purpose tool** is the king of all tools, the Swiss Army knife from which they all unfold. As ever, we are on a mission to discover *why* the writer has recorded this for us. What does he want us to understand or be startled by or rejoice in or weep over? So why does he record not one plague but ten? Presumably because that's how many there were in history! Yes, OK, but why in history was there not one plague but ten?

Here's a possible explanation – we'll call it 'the plan J hypothesis': God hoped to scare Pharaoh into submission with some blood, but he misjudged it. 'Hmm, blood didn't work,' thinks God. 'I'll try frogs.' But that fails too. And so do gnats. And so do flies. And so does killing the livestock. And so do boils. And so does hail. And so do locusts. And so does darkness. God fails nine times. But it's tenth time lucky. Finally he persuades Pharaoh to let his people go. Not so much plan A as plan J.

It would be a strange purpose, wouldn't it? To show us how unsuccessful God is in achieving his purposes. But the final judge of any interpretation must be the text itself. To the tools!

The first blade to fold out of your Swiss Army author's purpose knife is the **Structure tool**. When you read through Exodus 7 – 10 a couple times, you start to notice patterns in the plagues. See if you can spot them for yourself before you read on.

There's a pattern in the instructions Yahweh gives to Moses about whether or not he should warn Pharaoh about the forthcoming plague (and at what time of day):

'Go to Pharaoh in the morning' (plague 1)
  'Go in to Pharaoh' (plague 2)
    No warning (plague 3)

'Rise up early in the morning and present yourself to Pharaoh' (plague 4)
  'Go in to Pharaoh' (plague 5)
    No warning (plague 6)

'Rise up early in the morning and present yourself before Pharaoh' (plague 7)
  'Go in to Pharaoh' (plague 8)
    No warning (plague 9)

And there is a pattern in how each plague gets going:

Aaron stretches out his hand/staff (plague 1)
Aaron stretches out his hand/staff (plague 2)
Aaron stretches out his hand/staff (plague 3)

Yahweh starts the plague without the staff (plague 4)
Yahweh starts the plague without the staff (plague 5)
Moses starts the plague without the staff (plague 6)

Moses stretches out his hand/staff (plague 7)
Moses stretches out his hand/staff (plague 8)
Moses stretches out his hand (plague 9)

There's no point in using the **Structure tool** just to notice that plagues come in threes. We have to ask *why*? Why are the plagues arranged so intricately? Why does the author go out of his way to show us the beautifully crafted threefold cycles? At the very least, he's showing us that God is not trying a whole lot of different strategies at random. Something as carefully ordered as this must have been meticulously planned from the outset. The plan J hypothesis has hit an iceberg. One more tool will suffice to sink it.

Context tool
Read 4:21–23.

Which plague is alluded to in these verses?

How would you read the plagues differently in the context of 4:21–23? Is there ever any expectation that frogs, boils or hail will clinch it?

OK, so the plan J hypothesis is faring about as well as the *Titanic*. Obviously God intended ten plagues from the start. But we're still left answering the question 'why?' If God knew that only the death of the firstborn would break Pharaoh, why didn't he go for that plague to start with?

Here's a possible explanation: we'll call it 'the ten-plagues-for-ten-deities hypothesis'. It is often said that each of the plagues corresponds to a different Egyptian god or goddess, and that Yahweh despatches them one by one. Thus, the Egyptians worshipped the Nile god Hapi, and in the first plague Yahweh leaves him bleeding. They worshipped the goddess Heqet, writing her name in hieroglyphs with a little frog symbol, and in the second plague Yahweh leaves her hopping mad (Andrew apologizes for these puns which were Richard's idea!). They worshipped the Sun god Ra, and in the ninth plague Yahweh punches his lights out.

Though popular, this hypothesis leaves a bit to be desired. First, it doesn't explain why there were *ten* plagues – Wikipedia lists eighteen possible Egyptian deities! Secondly, some of the proposed god–plague connections become really tenuous, e.g. 'There was a plague of flies, and the god Khepri had a head of a . . . beetle.' Hmmm. Thirdly, and most importantly, nowhere *in the Bible text itself* does the author point us to this explanation.

Next up, the 'grind-Pharaoh-down hypothesis': Pharaoh is such a stubborn customer that even the death of the firstborn might not be enough to break him on its own. You have to chip away patiently over time. Accompanied by escalating horrors, God's command to 'Let my people go' comes a total of *seven* times. And little by little, Pharaoh's resistance weakens.

Number of plagues	'Let my people go' rating
0	'You must be joking, I don't even know who Yahweh is' (5:2).
1	
2	
3	
4	'OK, you can take the weekend off, but back to work on Monday' (8:28).
5	
6	
7	'I admit I've stuffed things up on this occasion' (9:27).
8	'The *men* can go, but leave the kids as a deposit so I know you're coming back' (10:8–11).
9	'You can all go – but I want your cattle' (10:24).
10	'GO!!!!!!!!!!!' (12:31).

The grind-Pharaoh-down hypothesis sounds very reasonable. But is this what the author is saying?

Repetition tool
Can you find the phrase that is repeated (with some minor variations) eighteen times in the book of Exodus and turns up especially often at the end of a plague episode?

Classify the different occurrences of this phrase. How many times does a) Yahweh do it, b) Pharaoh do it?

Having woven this phrase through his whole narrative, the author clearly intends it to guide our understanding. Does it support or overturn the grind-Pharaoh-down hypothesis?

If God's only plan is a quick rescue, why does he _____ Pharaoh's _____? (If you've done the exercise you'll be able to fill in the blanks.) Why, at just those points where it looks as though the whole thing is almost wrapped up, does God *deliberately* prolong things? Why, if God is trying to grind Pharaoh down, does he act to undermine the grinding-down process?

Part of the answer of course is that it's not all God's doing. Pharaoh _____ his own _____ plenty of times. There's no doubt that he is culpable. But that doesn't take away from the fact that God takes active steps to ensure that Pharaoh's _____ is just as _____ at the end of plague 9 as it was at the start of the whole show.[1]

Time for a brief aside on the subject of God's sovereignty and human free will. We can understand Pharaoh ending up at the spiritual cardiologist because of bad moral choices he's made – too much empire-building megalomania, too many baby-murdering psychopathic tendencies, too little regard for Yahweh. But when we discover that God has a hand in it, that God even *planned* it that way, we get confused. Does that mean that Pharaoh is just a pawn in God's chess game? Was it really Pharaoh's fault?

The Bible is clear: we are responsible for our actions *and* God is in control of them. We find this all over the place in Scripture. Out of jealousy, Joseph's brothers freely decided to sell him into slavery, yet God intended their action to save many lives (Genesis 50:20). Out of pride, the king of Assyria boasted in his plundering of Israel (Isaiah 10:7–11, 13–14), yet unbeknown to him he was acting as an instrument of God's judgment, an axe in God's hand (Isaiah 10:5–6, 15). Out of greed, Judas freely decided to betray Jesus for money (Matthew 26:14–16), yet God planned that Jesus should be betrayed to save many lives (Acts 2:23; 4:28). This is a big subject, and really worth exploring further. Here are a couple of books to add to your Amazon wish list:

- *A Call to Spiritual Reformation* by D. A. Carson (IVP) is the best thing we've read on prayer, with a helpful chapter on why we should pray to a God who is sovereign and has already decided what will happen. (All Don Carson's other books are good too!)
- *The Pleasures of God* by John Piper (Christian Focus) is an inspiringly God-centred book, and has a *really* good explanation of how God is sovereign in choosing who gets saved. (All John Piper's other books are good too!)

Back in Exodus, the point is the grind-Pharaoh-down hypothesis can't account for why God should want to _____

Pharaoh's _____. So we still haven't got to the bottom of the plagues.

With the first two avenues of investigation coming to nothing, we need to reach for the **Linking Words tool**. As we saw in the original *Dig Deeper*, linking words can help us to see the flow of an argument, revealing cause-and-effect relationships between different statements – just what we are looking for!

In the account of the first plague, before Moses announces that the Nile will turn to blood, the fish will die, the river will stink, etc., the author uses a linking word (see our italics) to tell us why:

> Thus says Yahweh, '*By this* you shall know that I am Yahweh: behold, with the staff that is in my hand I will strike the water that is in the Nile, and it shall turn into blood.'
> (7:17)

Toward the end of plague 2, Pharaoh pleads for the frogs to be taken away. Moses consents, but not without using another linking word.

> Moses said, 'Be it as you say, *so that* you may know that there is no one like Yahweh our God.'
> (8:10)

In plague 4, God explains that the insects will follow a restricted flight path. Look out for the linking word again:

> On that day I will set apart the land of Goshen, where my people dwell, so that no swarms of flies shall be there, *that* you may know that I am Yahweh in the midst of the earth.
> (8:22)

The plague of hail (number 7) goes linking-word-tastic. The plague comes '*so that* you may know that there is none like me in all the earth' (9:14). The plague ends '*so that* you may know that the earth is Yahweh's' (9:29). And in between we find out the entire point of Pharaoh's existence was to give Yahweh an opportunity to exercise his power '*so that* my name might be proclaimed in all the earth' (9:16; Paul also quotes this in Romans 9:17).

At the beginning of plague 8, God tells the Israelites to put this on the Sunday school syllabus. Another linking word:

> Tell in the hearing of your son and of your grandson how I have dealt harshly with the Egyptians and what signs I have done among them, *that* you may know that I am Yahweh.
> (10:2)

Now we know why there are ten plagues. Ten opportunities to watch Yahweh at work. He clicks his fingers, and water becomes blood. He has the frogs hopping to his music, the gnats dancing to his tune. He commands the weather. He turns off the sun with the ease of extinguishing a candle. And he will smash those who stand against him. Yahweh versus Pharaoh is not even worth a flutter with the bookies. They're not even taking bets.

It's worth an aside here on the Egyptian sorcerers. When Aaron throws down his staff and it turns into a snake, they are able to do the same (though Aaron's snake swallows their snakes). They succeed in copying Yahweh's water-to-blood trick – though you can't help thinking that Pharaoh would be more appreciative if they worked out how to turn some of the blood back to water! They also manage to summon some extra frogs. Like there weren't enough already. Thanks guys. (Do you get the impression that the author might be poking fun?) By the time we get to the Scottish plague, the magicians have given up. Yahweh's power is beyond them.

Do you remember 5:2? Pharaoh had no idea who Yahweh was. Ten plagues later and he's a little more enlightened. Yahweh is not a name you mess with. Opposing him is a monumentally foolish thing to do.

The same is true today. When a Cambodian dictator slaughters people made in his image, Yahweh won't stand for it. When Richard Dawkins writes a book arrogantly dismissing God as a delusion, Yahweh won't stand for it. When your nicest friend, loved by everyone and planning a career helping AIDS orphans, decides that Jesus isn't really for her, Yahweh won't stand for it.

The plagues are God's megaphone: 'I am Yahweh. Look what happens if you oppose me.'

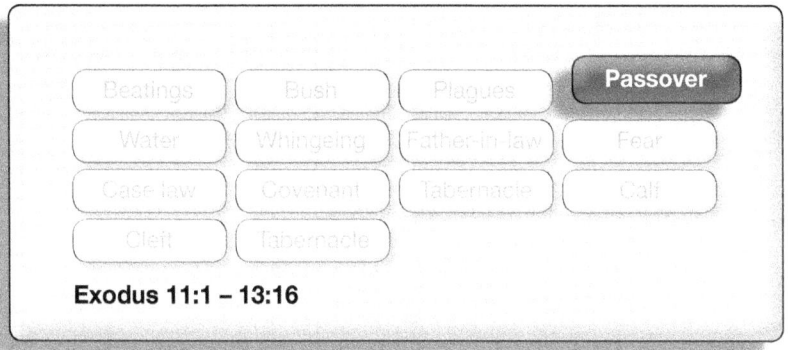

Exodus 11:1 – 13:16

Ten isn't in the three times table. Remembering from the last chapter that the plagues come in cycles of three, this simple bit of mental arithmetic tells you that the final plague stands alone. It sticks out like a sore thumb.

A closer look with the **Structure tool** reveals that plague 10 also breaks a pattern so obvious that you might not even have noticed it. Plagues 1–9 have a 'God promises, it happens' structure. He promises frogs; there are frogs. He promises darkness; there is darkness. And so on. But in the final plague the author breaks into the narrative between the plague and its fulfilment to give some unexpected directions about lambs and blood (12:1–28). The weird thing is, you almost wouldn't miss these verses if they weren't there. You could stop reading at 11:10 and pick up again at 12:29, and the story would make perfect sense. The sandwich structure is unique to plague number 10.

Instructions about lambs and blood (12:1–28) ⤵

God promises (11:1–10)	It happens (12:29–36)
The plague will happen at 'midnight' (11:4).	12:29
There will be a 'great cry throughout all the land of Egypt' (11:6).	12:30
Pharaoh's officials will tell the Israelites to 'get out' (11:8).	12:31–34
They should ask their neighbours for 'silver and gold jewellery' (11:2; cf. 3:22).	12:35–36

Exodus 11 – 12 is all about being rescued, but there are actually two rescues going on. There's a rescue *through* judgment and a rescue *from* judgment. God's people are rescued *through* God's judgment on Pharaoh – we find that on the outside of the sandwich, the bits of bread (11:1–10; 12:29–36). There we read of how God killed Pharaoh's firstborn son, the most devastating of all the plagues. This was the clincher, and as a result Pharaoh waved the white flag and let the people go. We'll come back to the rescue-through-judgment theme in the next chapter.

It is the filling of the sandwich that introduces the second theme: the rescue *from* judgment (12:1–28). There we read of how God's people are spared from the plague only by following instructions about lambs and blood. It comes as a surprise, because this is the first time that the Israelites have to *do* something to stay safe.

The US government has spent millions of pounds developing 'precision-guided munitions', aka smart bombs. Using laser guidance systems, or Global Positioning Systems, the idea is to create a weapon specific enough to take out the enemy missile launcher without flattening the primary school across the road. Tragically in modern conflicts they don't always succeed. But in ancient Egypt, God was already pretty good at it. The plagues were the ultimate smart weapon. Egyptian cows died, but Israelites' cows were left to eat grass in peace. Hailstones rained down everywhere except on the Israelite concentration camp in Goshen. God's people were even spared from the plague of darkness, for they 'had light where they lived' (10:23). Twice the author describes the underlying principle: 'Yahweh will make a distinction between . . . Israel and . . . Egypt' (9:4; cf. 11:7).

This time the distinction isn't automatic. There are instructions about lambs and blood. Something has to be *done*, to avert the judgment. The verses at the heart of the sandwich are going to tell us the heart of the gospel.

Polar bears and ketchup sachets
The instructions about lambs and blood go a bit like this. You take a lamb into your household on the tenth day of the month (12:3). The children play with it, cuddle it at bedtimes, give it the pet name 'Shaun'. Four days later Shaun gets slaughtered (crying children), his blood gets spread all over the doorposts, and everyone sits down to a roast dinner. At midnight, while everyone is tucked up in bed, God '[strikes] down all the firstborn in the land of Egypt, from the firstborn of Pharaoh who sat on his throne to the firstborn of the captive who was in the dungeon' (12:29). But the Israelite children sleep safe in their beds. God has made a distinction, but only because of the blood. As he promised, 'when I see the blood, I will pass over you'

(12:13). And so they called it the Passover. They have now been celebrating it for over 3,000 years.

I (Andrew) have done a few youth talks on this chapter. First time, managed to find a soft toy lamb in a second-hand shop, stuffed it with sachets of tomato ketchup from a motorway service station. Bob was my uncle. Did it a few more times. Couldn't find a toy lamb, so tried to explain to more than a thousand teenagers why a fluffy polar bear was a close approximation. Did it again on a youth weekend away in Scarborough and had completely forgotten to pack the requisite toy in my suitcase. Sent the teenagers round town in the afternoon on a 'find-the-cutest-soft-toy-you-can-for-a-pound' competition. Little did they realize my ultimate intentions. Pictures of me wielding a huge knife and looking like a psycho ended up on Facebook.

Teenagers (or at least the boys) loved the blood and gore of the re-enactment. But the original must have been a very solemn occasion. Imagine, you're woken up in the night by screams from next door. Then there's another cry from across the road. And another from down the street. Your heart starts to beat faster. You wonder what's going on. You go to check on the children . . .

It was a night of utter tragedy and devastation, the darkest episode in the history of a nation. The cry uttered was 'such as there has never been, nor ever will be again' (11:6). And no wonder, 'for there was not a house where someone was not dead' (12:30). There is nothing more terrifying than the judgment of God. And yet the chapter is quite clear: unless there is a sacrifice, this judgment will fall on God's people no less than on their oppressors.

If we reflect for a moment on the cruelty of Pharaoh's regime, the horror of the Egyptian concentration camp, the brutality of his edict to kill the babies for no better reason than his own insecurity, well then maybe we understand something of God's righteous anger at evil, the 'rightness' of his judgment. But we struggle when we think of God punishing 'nice people'; we struggle when we think of God being angry with us. That's because we divide the world into goodies and baddies. Pharaoh comes on stage and we boo like in a panto. But we, like the Israelites, are the goodies. We think we should be spared.

But the Bible doesn't share our pantomime-view of the world. It's easy to read the opening chapters of Exodus with a rose-tinted view of the Israelites, as if they were only innocent victims. Later chapters will reveal that they can be just as hard-hearted as Pharaoh. They will grumble against God in the desert. They will turn aside from him to worship a golden calf. The thing that makes the difference between the Israelites and Egyptians on Passover night isn't that some are good and some are bad. The difference is that some have blood on the door and some don't.

You can be fairly sure that an Israelite, on the night of the first Passover, is not going to forget to kill the lamb. Picture the scene:

> Eldest son: Have you done it yet, Dad?
> Father: Sure son. Relax. I'll do it at half time.
> *Some time passes.*
> Eldest son: Have you done it yet, Dad?
> Father: Yes, son. I promise I'll do it as soon as the match finishes.
> *More time passes.*
> Eldest son: Have you done it yet, Dad?
> Father: Sorry, son – it went into extra time! I'll do it before the highlights.

It's not very likely is it? The blood is going to be on the doorposts before anyone even thinks of football, and certainly before any eldest sons get a wink of sleep. And we're not talking a dab of blood here and there. The whole front of the house is going to be *doused* in the stuff. (This was an aspect of the story to which we were faithful in our tomato ketchup re-enactment!)

It's simple. The lamb dies. An Israelite boy lives. It's what theologians call 'penal substitution' – 'penal' meaning that we face God's judgment; 'substitution' meaning that this judgment is borne by someone else in our place. All very interesting as a history lesson. There was a night in the second millennium BC when it was quite important for Israelite families living in Egypt to kill lambs. But what does it mean for us today?

There are a few tools that can help with the 'what-does-this-then-have-to-say-to-me-now' type questions, namely:

Quotation/Allusion
Copycat
Bible Timeline
Who am I?

If you were working on your own, you would need to try all of these tools, to see which was the most help. But because you're reading a nice book, we're going to be friendly and give you a hint, and whisper in your ear, 'Try the **Quotation/Allusion tool**.'

Quotation/Allusion Tool
Read Luke's account of the Last Supper in the New Testament (Luke 22:7–22).

What's the connection between these verses and the events of Exodus 12? (Hint: the **Repetition tool** might also be helpful here.)

Why might Luke want to make such a connection, as he begins his description of the events leading up to Jesus' death?

What would be the equivalent for us of putting blood on the doorposts?

What would you say to the person who wants to finish watching the footie before they bother to sort it out?

Keep a thumb in Luke 22, as we'll be coming back shortly . . .

A knot in the handkerchief
Salvation from God's judgment through the blood of a substitute is something Yahweh doesn't want the Israelites ever to forget.

For starters, they need a new calendar: 'This month shall be for you the beginning of months. It shall be the first month of the year for you' (12:2). Imagine that! After the Passover the Israelites all had to get new diaries – great news for the Egyptian branch of WH Smith. Just as we divide history into BC and AD, they would have divided it into BP ('before Passover') and AP. Every date in Israelite history looked back to the saving death of a lamb.

Then there are the festivals. The first date to write in their new diary is the 14th of the month. That's the Passover feast. It's roast lamb every year from now on. And God has designed it as the first ever Sunday school teaching aid:

> And when you come to the land that Yahweh will give you, as he has promised, you shall keep this service. And when your children say to you, 'What do you mean by this service?' you shall say, 'It is the sacrifice of Yahweh's Passover, for he passed over the houses of the people of Israel in Egypt, when he struck the Egyptians but spared our houses.'
>
> (12:25–27a)

Although this happened every year, the Bible draws particular attention to Passover celebrations at the big turning points in the nation's history: just before they set out from Mount Sinai; just before the walls of Jericho fell; at the time of national reforms by Hezekiah and Josiah; immediately after the return from exile; and of course in an upper room in Jerusalem with a Jewish carpenter and twelve friends (Numbers 9:1–14; Joshua 5:10–11; 2 Kings 23:21–23; 2 Chronicles 30:1–5; 35:1–13; Ezra 6:19–21; Luke 22:7–22).

Immediately after the Passover came the week-long Feast of Unleavened [made without yeast] Bread (12:14–20; 13:3–10). This commemorated the hasty flight from Egypt, because on the first Passover they escaped in the middle of the night before there was time to let the bread rise.

But the most vivid of all the ceremonies associated with Passover was the redemption of the firstborn son (13:1–2, 11–16). Every firstborn had to be either killed or redeemed with the blood of a lamb. Again, God is particularly concerned for the Christian education of the children (parents take note):

> And when in time to come your son asks you, 'What does this mean?' you shall say to him, 'By a strong hand Yahweh brought us out of Egypt, from the house of slavery. For when Pharaoh

stubbornly refused to let us go, Yahweh killed all the firstborn in the land of Egypt, both the firstborn of man and the firstborn of animals. Therefore I sacrifice to Yahweh all the males that first open the womb, but all the firstborn of my sons I redeem.'
(13:14–15)

But what about us? We don't use the Jewish calendar; some of us are vegetarians and don't eat lamb; Hovis doesn't do an unleavened variety, and the only ceremony our firstborn gets is a baby shower. Does that mean we can forget the Passover?

(Dig Deeper)

Quotation/Allusion tool
Read Luke's account of the Last Supper (Luke 22:7–22) again. The Passover was a one-off event, but remembered every year at the Passover festival. Similarly, Jesus' death on the cross for our sins was a one-off event. But how does Jesus want it to be remembered?

How does your increased understanding of Exodus help you to appreciate the significance of the 'Lord's Supper' or 'Holy Communion'?

BRAINBOX ASIDE: Firstborn whom?
For whom is the lamb a substitute? Is it (a) the eldest boy? (b) the whole household? or (c) the whole nation?

On first glance you'd say (a). The eldest son is the one who faces death at midnight. He's the one spared from the plague when Yahweh sees the blood. He's the one involved in the ceremony of the redemption of the firstborn.

But why then is it necessary to select a lamb according to the size and appetites of the *household* (12:2–4)? That seems to favour (b). And how come it's OK to share a lamb with next door? Could you end up with one lamb for two firstborns?

Now check out 4:22–23. This seems to be a prediction, in miniature, of the whole Passover story, but here Yahweh describes the whole nation of Israel as 'my firstborn son'. Now (c) is getting some votes!

We're not going to give you all the answers, partly because we don't know them! We just want to show you that the Bible has always got more to tell us. It's always stretching our understanding. We've never got it taped.

Happy digging!

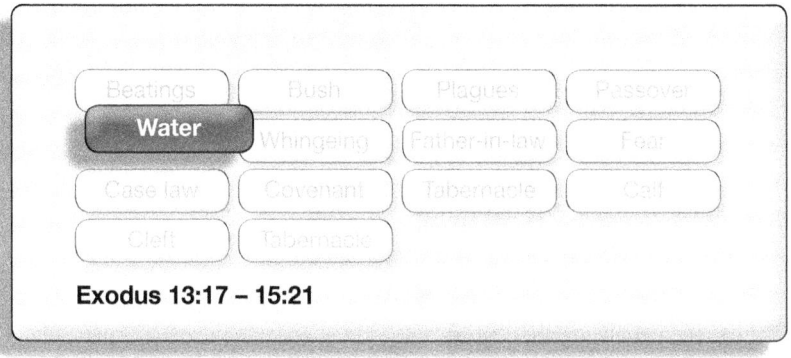

Exodus 13:17 – 15:21

Well, here we are. It's already time for the parting of the Red Sea. If you ever get the chance to make *Exodus: The Movie*, you'll want to save most of your special-effects budget for this moment. A corridor of air cut out of the sea with sheer walls of water on either side; a chase scene involving the entire Egyptian army complete with chariots – this is going to make even *The Battle of Helm's Deep* look small-scale.

The narrative doesn't start there, however. Before we arrive at the sea, we hear about the journey through the desert (13:17–22). This isn't an air-conditioned coach tour of the Pyramids. We're talking long-distance walk through sandstorms with constant risk of death by dehydration. Our guess is you pack light: some sunscreen, a hat, and as much water as you can carry. The one thing you don't pack is the container with the bones of your great, great uncle (13:19)! Or do you? You just have to ask, *'Why is Moses travelling with a coffin?'* And why does the writer feel the need to tell us about it?

Quotation/Allusion tool
Read Exodus 13:19. The narrator explains why Moses is packing bones by quoting some words from the end of Genesis.

Look up the original context of the quotation in Genesis 50:24–25. Do you understand now why the author of Exodus chose to mention the bones? How does this seemingly random detail serve to underline one of the main themes of Exodus?

The Pharaoh strikes back

Judging from the way this section starts, you would think that everything is sorted: 'When Pharaoh let the people go . . .' (13:17). Moses has been pleading to be 'let go' since 5:1, and at times it seemed as if it would never happen. But now, ten plagues later, Pharaoh has come to his senses. The Israelites are no longer slaves. They are walking free in the desert, with Egypt in the rear-view mirror and a pillar of cloud and fire out in front. And they all lived happily ever after.

Not quite.

The first hint of trouble comes in 14:2 when God says, 'Turn back.' Then in verse 5 Pharaoh has a sudden change of heart: 'What is this we have done, that we have let Israel go from serving us?'. By verse 6, he's strapped into his chariot and marshalling the Egyptian army. Some people, it seems, don't know when to give up.

He quickly assembles a crack squadron of highly trained troops (verse 7), and they set off in hot pursuit (verse 8). By verse 9, not only has he caught up with the Israelites, he's pulled off a spectacular military manoeuvre: the Israelites are trapped, with the Egyptians on one side, the Red Sea on the other.

The Israelites are quick to abandon all trust in God (verses 10–12), a nasty habit of theirs that we'll come back to in the next chapter. But as we readers know, this is all in God's plan. God dangles the Israelites in front of Pharaoh's nose like the artificial rabbit on a greyhound track, enticing Pharaoh to chase them. And all for a reason that should be quite familiar by now:

> And I will harden Pharaoh's heart, and he will pursue them, and I will get glory over Pharaoh and all his host, and the Egyptians *shall know that I am Yahweh.*
> (14:4)

In fact this is so important, that the author says it again (**Repetition tool** alert!) a few verses later:

> And I will harden the hearts of the Egyptians so that they shall go in after them, and I will get glory over Pharaoh and all his host, his chariots, and his horsemen. And the Egyptians *shall know that I am Yahweh*, when I have gained glory over Pharaoh, his chariots, and his horsemen.
> (14:17–18)

Here is the theme tune of Exodus, something we hear again and again through the book. Yahweh is passionately concerned that people know his name, and what his name stands for. Here, in these chapters, Yahweh is revealed as a warrior who smashes his enemies with terrifying ease.

Please read through chapter 14 yourself. Read it as a narrative of actual events, every bit as historical as the Battle of Hastings or Neil Armstrong's first steps on the moon. Read it in the knowledge that one day you will have the opportunity of meeting some of the people who were there! I can't wait to hear from them first-hand how their sandals stayed dry as they stepped apprehensively between the walls of water. Read it and try to picture the sheer scale of the Egyptian army: 600+ chariots funnelling into the sea-passageway as they give chase. Read it and discover the origin of the popular phrase: 'the wheels . . . come off' (verse 25). Read of the water crashing down and sweeping away 'all the host of Pharaoh' (verse 28). Read it and wonder at the 'great power' of Yahweh, and join the Israelites in fearing him (verse 31).

Unsurprisingly, some people get into a flap about whether it's allowed for water to stand up as a wall without being frozen. Cambridge University Professor Colin Humphreys tackles this head-on in *The Miracles of Exodus* (2003), in which he tries to reassure us that everything has a 'rational explanation'. For example, the burning bush is a venting of volcanic gas; the sea turns blood-red because of toxic algae; the plague of hail leaves behind damp sand, ideal egg-laying conditions for locusts. Locust droppings later contaminate the grain, which then poisons the Egyptian firstborn. And something called 'wind setdown' parts the Red Sea. *Titanic* Director James Cameron goes for something similar in his 2006 film, *The Exodus Decoded*.

Hats off to the professor for ingenuity! He's bending over backwards to keep the events of the Exodus (which he accepts as true) within the boundaries set by the laws of physics. But we're not so sure that God always has to stick to the rules – what about the resurrection of Jesus? And Professor Humphrey's explanations don't always stick as closely as they might to the biblical text. For example, his account of why the Israelite firstborn survived the tenth plague makes no reference to lambs (he suggests their grain stores were not contaminated with mycotoxins!). And while 'wind setdown' could perhaps *lower* the sea-level on either side of a raised causeway, it certainly wouldn't produce a 'wall of water' on both sides (14:22). On a youth group weekend away, Andrew tested the wind theory with a bowl of water and some hairdryers. Suffice to say that the effect wasn't very Exodus-like!

The fact is that God parted the waters of the Red Sea. It was a miracle. Whether God did it by using a spare volcano and 'wind setdown', or by just temporarily altering the properties of water molecules in a way that gives scientists a headache, doesn't really matter. It was a very powerful thing to do. But Yahweh doesn't seem to find it difficult. Just as it was no trouble for him to un-part the waters and drown a whole army.

The events of chapter 14 tell us that Yahweh is not a name to be trifled with. It's not a good idea to pick a fight with him. If you do, you're going to lose.

Karaoke night

As we move from chapter 14 to chapter 15, we need to reach for the **Genre tool**. As we saw in the original *Dig Deeper*, there are many different genres in the Bible: songs, prophecies, proverbs, laments, visions, speeches, parables, historical narrative, for example. Identifying the genre is very important to how we interpret a passage.

Exodus 14 is narrative. Exodus 15:1–18 is a poem. The difference in genre is important. If we treat chapter 14 as a poem, we might downplay the historicity of the events, forgetting that they *actually took place*. But if we stay in factual, it-happened-just-like-this mode when we come to Exodus 15, then some of the language is going to tie us in knots. Verse 7 tells us that that the Egyptians were burned like stubble, but it's hard to imagine how they caught fire with so much water around! As historical description it's awkward; as a poem it's a vivid way of describing their untimely end, together with being 'swallowed' and 'thrown into the sea' and dropping to the bottom 'like lead' or 'like a stone'.

For some reason, at this point in Exodus the biblical author decided to switch to poetry. It wasn't enough just to tell us what happened. Now he wants to drive the message home in a way that resonates with our emotions and gets our hearts pumping faster. It ought to get us reaching into the toolbox again, this time for the **Tone and Feel tool**. And it's over to you again.

Tone and Feel tool
Read 15:1–21 again.

How is this making you feel? Is the tone of the passage most like:
  a) A BBC news bulletin reporting on a military defeat?.
  b) Football fans taunting the other team after a 4–0 lead?
  c) A relieved schoolgirl telling her mum about her narrow escape from a bully?

Think first about the kind of imagery that the author uses. How would he complete the sentence: 'God's victory over the Egyptians was like . . . '?

Now focus on the verbs in verses 9–10. It takes six verbs to narrate the Egyptians' boasting, but only one to describe Yahweh's response. What effect does this convey?

Why do you think the author has chosen to describe the response of Israel's *future* enemies in verses 14–16?

> (We won't meet the Moabites, Edomites or Canaanites until the book of Numbers.) How does this contribute to the sense of confidence?
>
> What does the use of tambourines and dancing (verse 20) tell you about the tone and feel of the passage? How about the repeated chorus in verse 21?

You can imagine 'The Horse and His Rider' going straight to number one in the charts. It was so catchy that people could still remember the words at the time of Jeremiah nearly 800 years later (Jeremiah 51:21; see also Haggai 2:22, even later still). It's obvious that it's a very happy song. But maybe we're a little taken aback by exactly what makes them so happy.

Are they celebrating their escape from slavery? Well yes, partly.

Are they celebrating the laws-of-physics-bending abilities of God? A bit perhaps.

Are they celebrating the way that God smashed their enemies? Are they chuffed that God picked up the horse and his rider and hurled them into the sea? Yes. That's the one. They are celebrating, first and foremost, God's overthrow of the Egyptians. And perhaps that comes as a surprise.

The idea that God will one day judge the world and punish those who oppose him is taught throughout the Bible, not least by Jesus. Often we think of this as the 'bad news', in contrast to the 'good news' that Jesus can save us. But Miriam and her dancing companions include the judgment bit under the 'good news' heading. And they're right.

It is good news that God will destroy evil and punish wrongdoing. We're rightly appalled when a lax judge at the Old Bailey lets off a serial rapist with no more than a caution. But imagine if the moral guardian of the universe was similarly laid back about justice: 'Hi Pharaoh. Why are you looking so nervous? Oh, the drowning-Israelite-babies-in-the-Nile thing? Oh, don't worry too much about that. Let's pretend it never happened. Welcome to paradise.' Maybe some people have a fluffy, cotton-wool-clad Santa-god like that. But it's not Yahweh. Yahweh repays people according to what they have done (cf. Romans 2:5–6). Those who have drowned babies in the river he drowns in the sea.

God's judgment on Pharaoh saves the Israelites. Only now can they rest in peace, without the constant fear of chariots over the brow of every hill. At the Passover they were saved *from* God's judgment by the blood of a lamb. But at the Red Sea they are saved *through* God's judgment – it is the defeat of their enemies that wins their freedom.

	Danger facing Israelites	**Means of rescue**
Salvation from judgment	Judgment of God	Passover lamb
Salvation through judgment	Tyranny of Pharaoh	Drowning of Egyptians

But now we need to ask, what does this have to say to me in the twenty-first century? God saved the Israelites by drowning their oppressor, so does that mean God is going to throw my annoying boss into a lake on his commute to work? Can we expect similar treatment for perpetrators of genocide in Africa? Or for sweatshop owners in Asia or human traffickers in Europe? We need to be very careful here, and reach first for the **Bible Timeline tool**. Does anything change as we move from Old Testament to New Testament?

In the Exodus, God's people were slaves in a physical country (Egypt) under a human tyrant (Pharaoh). In the New Testament, the emphasis is not on slavery to a political power, but slavery to sin (e.g. Ephesians 2:1–3; John 8:34), and our oppressor is ultimately a spiritual one (Ephesians 2:2; John 8:44). Accordingly, Jesus wasn't interested in overthrowing Caesar – he told people to pay their taxes – and he refused to engage in a political or military struggle:

> My kingdom is not of this world. If my kingdom were of this world, my servants would have been fighting, that I might not be delivered over to the Jews. But my kingdom is not from the world. (John 18:36)

So how is the conquest aspect of the Exodus story fulfilled in Jesus? Referring to his coming death, he explained that 'now will the ruler of this world [the devil] be cast out' (John 12:31). The apostle John later explained that 'the reason the Son of God appeared was to destroy the works of the devil' (1 John 3:8). So the drowning of the Egyptians in the Red Sea prefigures the defeat of Satan at the cross, and the rescue of Christians from his grip.

That doesn't mean that God is unconcerned about ongoing political and social oppression today. He promises that one day he will judge our human enemies as well as our spiritual ones (indeed they may sometimes be connected): 'to repay with affliction those who afflict you and . . . inflict vengeance on those who do not know God' (2 Thessalonians 1:6–8; cf. Romans 12:19). So as well as the Red Sea fulfilment at the cross, when Satan is defeated, there is another Red Sea moment to come, as all of those opposed to God are swept away at the final judgment.

Tragically, some have hijacked the Exodus motif in Scripture to create a theology that is all about political freedom and nothing to do with salvation from sin. In 1968, the World Council of Churches agreed that the mission of God was being fulfilled in 'the emancipation of coloured races, the concern for the humanisation of industrial relations, [and] various attempts at rural development . . . '. The current social problems of the world had so filled their horizon that they completely forgot that above all else we need to be rescued from a future judgment.

Where does that leave Christian social and political involvement? As evangelicals, we should be proud of the heritage of men like William Wilberforce whose tireless parliamentary campaigning finally brought about the end of the British slave trade, or Lord Shaftsbury who introduced (amongst other things) the 1833 Factory Act, limiting working hours for children. Those who love the gospel have always loved justice. But their first passion will always be to see people 'delivered . . . from the domain of darkness and transferred . . . to the kingdom of his beloved Son, in whom we have redemption, the forgiveness of sins' (Colossians 1:13–14).

> O come, Thou Rod of Jesse, free
> Thine own from Satan's tyranny.
> From depths of Hell Thy people save
> And give them victory o'er the grave.
> Rejoice! Rejoice! Emmanuel
> Shall come to thee, O Israel.[1]

BRAINBOX ASIDE: How many shadows?
Pizza Express is the best. Granted it costs twice as much as Pizza Hut, but you get posher ingredients like Parma ham and

asparagus, and – here's the key thing – it has the coolest halogen spotlights. Many an evening has Andrew spent eating his *bruschetta con funghi*, seeing how many simultaneous shadows he can cast with a single finger. Current record stands at five.

Important events in the Bible cast shadows too – for example, Jesus' rescue mission is foreshadowed in the crossing of the sea. But just as in Pizza Express, there is more than one shadow to be found by those who look closely.

Moses led God's people out of Egypt, but it was his successor, Joshua, who took them into the Promised Land. What Red-Sea-crossing shadows can you find in Joshua 2:8–13 and 3:14–17 and 5:1? Look closely! There may be more connections than you think. Why do you think the author wants to tie these events and these people together in our minds?

If Moses and Joshua form a bit of a double act, then so do the prophets Elijah and Elisha. What Red-Sea-crossing shadows can you find in 2 Kings 2? Why do you think the author makes these associations?

How is our understanding that Jesus fulfils the Exodus story deepened by throwing Joshua, Elijah and Elisha into the mix?

Happy digging!

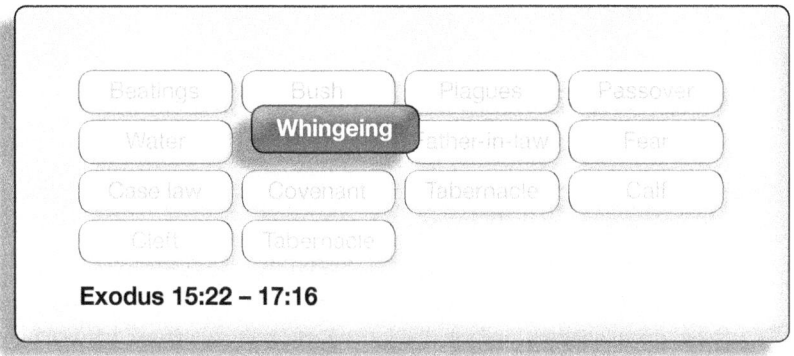

Exodus 15:22 – 17:16

This is the kind of chapter that, if it were a football match, would have you shouting at the telly. If it were word-processing software, it would give you repetitive strain injury from pressing Ctrl-Z ('undo'). Expect tears of frustration.

So far in Exodus we've mainly learned lessons about Yahweh: what his name means and what it stands for. It was more about Yahweh than it was about us. The other key characters to date have been Pharaoh and Moses. They weren't models for us either. No-one wants to be like Pharaoh, and the **Who am I? tool** warned us not to step too quickly into Moses' shoes – we haven't had a burning-bush experience!

In this chapter, it is the ordinary people of God who take centre stage. Here there is a real possibility of reading ourselves into the story. Indeed, the **Who am I? tool** might even encourage it – they have been rescued by the blood of the lamb just as we have been rescued by the blood of Jesus; they are on their way to the Promised Land just as we are heading for the promised new creation. The Israelite is the equivalent of the Christian. In some ways this is a chapter about us (or people very like us).

OK, so we've found some normal Christians in the book of Exodus. We can identify with them. Now we need to use the **Copycat tool** to establish how their example applies to us. The first stage is to ask whether the author is *prescribing* their behaviour or merely *describing* it? Just because he tells us that the Israelites survived on a diet of edible dew doesn't mean he wants us to do the same! In some ways, the Israelites' experience is a one-off.

In other ways, their experience parallels ours. That brings us to the second stage in using the **Copycat tool**. We need to work out whether the author is holding them up as a positive example or a negative one. Some examples in the Bible are worth imitating, others are best avoided.

Sit in your favourite armchair. Dim the lights. Make a cup of camomile tea. Get a wet towel ready, should it become necessary to wrap it around your head. And begin reading one of the most exasperating sections of the Old Testament.

Muppetry

So basically it goes a bit like this. The Israelites finish their 'Horse-and-His-Rider' karaoke night and head off into the desert in high spirits. They travel for three days without coming across any water and so must have been pretty relieved to find some at Marah. Unfortunately it's undrinkable, and their confidence in Yahweh's faithfulness evaporates. They grumble against Moses. Amazingly, at Yahweh's instruction, Moses chucks in a piece of special wood, and the bitter water turns into lemonade. Next stop Elim, where the water supply is so lavish ('twelve springs and seventy palm trees', 15:27) that they must have been rather embarrassed to have doubted Yahweh's provision.

They travel a little further and can't find any food. Their confidence in Yahweh's faithfulness evaporates. They grumble against Moses and Aaron. Amazingly, Yahweh feeds them with bread from heaven and quails (posh chickens – if you're a Gordon Ramsay fan you'll know all about them). Red faces all round for having doubted Yahweh again.

Next they reach Rephidim where there's no water. But that's OK, because we know by now that Yahweh is faithful, and he always provides, and there's no need to doubt him at all, and . . . guys, come on . . . No, you can't be serious . . .

> The people thirsted there for water, and the people grumbled against Moses and said, 'Why did you bring us up out of Egypt, to kill us and our children and our livestock with thirst?'
> (17:3)

Amazingly, at Yahweh's instruction, Moses takes the same staff with which he struck the Nile (which ironically caused a water *shortage* in the first plague) and strikes a rock, causing water to burst forth.

The **Repetition tool** takes us straight to the point: The Israelites grumble. Yahweh is faithful. The Israelites grumble. Yahweh is faithful. The Israelites grumble. Yahweh is faithful.

Tone and Feel tool
Read Exodus 16 again.

Yahweh is faithful. But how do the *details* of the narrative paint his faithfulness in glorious Technicolor?

> The Israelites are idiots. Score out of ten their ability to follow simple instructions concerning a) when to collect manna, b) when to store manna overnight.
>
> How does the author's mention of bad smells and maggots help you to feel the point?

The faithfulness of Yahweh is so remarkable that some of the manna gets put in a jam jar as a memento of the heavenly feeding; something for the grandchildren to ask about, an unforgettable symbol of Yahweh's faithfulness (16:32–36).

Uncomfortably for the Israelites, it's their *lack of faith* that gets commemorated. They tested Yahweh (an irony in itself since *they* were the ones who were supposed to be being tested, 15:25), and so one of the staging posts on their journey gets called Massah, meaning 'testing'; another is called Meribah, meaning 'quarrelling' (17:7). Not the first time in Exodus that names have had meanings, but by far the most embarrassing to date. Imagine taking a taxi home:

> 'Where to, guv'nor?'
> 'Whingeton-on-Sea.'
> 'Oh yeah, I know it guv'nor, right bunch of misery-guts live there. What road?'
> 'I-was-a-right-idiot-for-doubting-Yahweh Avenue'
> 'Right you are.'

It would burn the lesson into your memory wouldn't it? The Israelites are as much to be desired as role models as Lawrence 'Lawn Chair Larry' Walters (Google him). As one of Andrew's mum's teacher friends once said rather unkindly of her students,

'If their brains were dynamite, they wouldn't even light their eyes up.'

Of course we'd never be that daft. None of us, having been rescued by God at the price of his Son's life, would ever doubt his love for us in difficult times. None of us, with the confident hope of a future resurrection, would ever be shaken by momentary affliction.

Or would we?

Do you see how the author has achieved his purpose? We read the narrative of the Israelites and we cannot believe the extent of their muppetry. We want to shout at them, 'Come on! You *cannot* be that stupid!' And then we realize the author has tricked us, Nathan-the-prophet style (2 Samuel 12:1–7). We find that we are rebuking ourselves.

The **Quotation/Allusion tool** confirms that we are thinking along the right lines. Exodus 17 is part of a bewildering web of interconnected passages that culminates in a direct application to New Testament believers:[1]

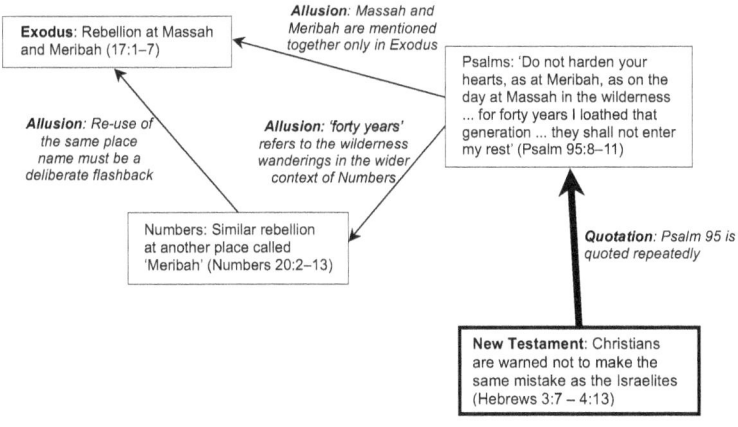

Figure 1

Don't worry if you don't follow it all. The take-home message (from Exodus 17, via Psalm 95 and Hebrews 3 – 4) is simple: Don't do what the Israelites did. Don't harden your heart.

The Amalekite conundrum
When it comes to the **Author's Purpose tool**, the skill that sets the master craftsman apart from the cowboy is *evaluation*. The first interpretation you think of isn't necessarily the right one. Nor is the first answer that someone gives in your Bible study. Both have to be weighed and tested against the benchmark of the text. Often, like Wile E. Coyote, we will have to go 'back to the drawing board' again and again. We keep reading, keep praying, keep digging deeper until we get it. Suddenly it clicks. We had that kind of experience when we asked, 'Why was there not one plague but ten?' a few chapters back. The conundrum of the Amalekites poses a similar challenge.

Why does the author tell us about the Amalekites? (Read Exodus 17:8–16 again to refresh your memory.) One answer might be: for historical completeness. These marauding villains turned up at Rephidim, and the author felt duty-bound to chronicle the facts. Fair enough. Except that, like all Bible narrators, he is a theologian as well as a historian, and he is deliberately selective about what he chooses to include and what he leaves out. What is his *purpose* then in leaving this in?

First up, the 'lift-up-your-hands-in-church' hypothesis. The question of whether you should raise your hands in worship has vexed the church down through the years. In some churches, anything less than 80° elevation during the chorus is seen as half-hearted; in others, eyebrows will be raised as soon as hands leave the safety of the chino pockets where they are thought to belong! So it's a good thing that here in Exodus the dispute is resolved once and for all: lift your hands in church and you'll keep winning your spiritual battles!

You don't need us to spell out the problems with this theory. You can use the **Who am I? tool** for yourself by now. Enough said.

Next up, the 'Amalekites-are-bad-dudes' hypothesis. (Thanks to our American friend Jed for this terminology.) This is our first encounter with one of Israel's historic enemies – they show up later in battles with Gideon, Samuel and King David amongst others – but they're particularly unwelcome at this point. After 430 years in Egypt (12:40) and less than three months of freedom (19:1), the sight of Amalek on the horizon ready to enslave you all over again is not a happy one. The Israelites are defenceless refugees; it is a cruel time to strike.

According to the 'Amalekites-are-bad-dudes' hypothesis, the author's purpose is to show us that the Amalekites must be blotted out (17:14). This even gets written down on a scroll as a guide for future military commanders, not least Joshua (mentioned three times here, the guy who goes on to lead the conquest of the Promised Land). You see an Amalekite on the horizon? Pull the trigger. The Amalekites are bad dudes.

The **Quotation/Allusion tool** provides some support for this theory, for this Exodus passage is quoted in Deuteronomy 25:17–19. The point is exactly the same. They are bad dudes, and their memory must be blotted out from under heaven:

> Remember what Amalek did to you on the way as you came out of Egypt, how he attacked you on the way when you were faint and weary, and cut off your tail, those who were lagging behind you, and he did not fear God. Therefore when Yahweh your God

has given you rest from all your enemies around you, in the land that Yahweh your God is giving you for an inheritance to possess, you shall blot out the memory of Amalek from under heaven; you shall not forget.
(Deuteronomy 25:17–19; see also 1 Samuel 15:2–3)

Certainly the 'bad-dudes' hypothesis is doing better than the 'lift-your-hands' one. It's definitely partly right. And yet we still felt uneasy about signing off on it. For one thing, it's not obvious what it has to teach us today. But the other reason for our unease was the **Context tool**: what has this got to do with the Israelites whingeing? Is this new episode really completely unconnected to what has gone before?

Context tool

Look at the immediate context of 17:7. How does the Amalekite episode help to answer the Israelites' question?

The **Context tool** leads us to the 'Yahweh-is-faithful' hypothesis. You know you're on to something when all the bits of the passage start to fit together and point in the same direction. We've already noticed Moses' raised hands, but we didn't mention what they were holding – his staff. That should get bells ringing. Moses' hands and staff are of great significance in the wider context of the book. The staff/hands combination triggered several of the plagues (e.g. 9:23; 10:13), divided the Red Sea (14:16), and caused water to spring forth from the rock (17:5–6). The staff/hands combination represents God's activity through Moses, so much so that . . . Check out who was holding the staff back in 7:17:

> Thus says Yahweh, 'By this you shall know that I am Yahweh: behold, with the staff that is in *my* hand I will strike the water that is in the Nile, and it shall turn into blood.'
> (7:17)

Moses' staff and hands are the agents of Yahweh. When Moses lowers his hands, Israel loses (17:11). When he lifts his hands 'upon the throne of Yahweh' – a symbol of prayerful dependence (17:16; see also 1 Timothy 2:8) – Israel wins. The point is clear, and it ought to be sinking in by now. Yahweh is with his people; he never leaves them. He is utterly faithful. You would have to be a complete muppet to stop trusting him.

> **BRAINBOX ASIDE: Travelling rocks**
> Moses strikes a rock to find water at Horeb (17:6) at the beginning of the Israelites' journey through the wilderness. He does something similar at Kadesh at the *end* of their desert travels (Numbers 20:11). You might think that these are two similar water-yielding rocks in different places, but in 1 Corinthians 10:4, Paul tells us that the one rock 'followed them'. A miraculous travelling rock? Paul explains further that 'the rock was Christ'.
>
> Some scholars take this *typologically*, meaning that God's provision of water to thirsty people in the desert is analogous to the gift of his Son to the spiritually thirsty (more on typology when we come to look at the tabernacle). Others take it *literally*, meaning that Jesus really was travelling with them in the desert disguised as a rock.
>
> Which one do you think Paul means? Rather than just picking which theory you prefer, look in the texts and their contexts (Exodus, Numbers and 1 Corinthians) for clues.

> The 'spiritual drink' in 1 Corinthians 10:4 is paralleled with 'spiritual food', presumably referring to the manna. How does the relationship between Jesus and the manna (and here you have some other passages to help you, e.g. John 6) enable you to decide about the connection between Jesus and the rock?
>
> How do these observations illuminate your understanding of the central themes of Exodus 15:22 – 17:16, namely God's faithfulness and our lack of faith?
>
> Happy digging!

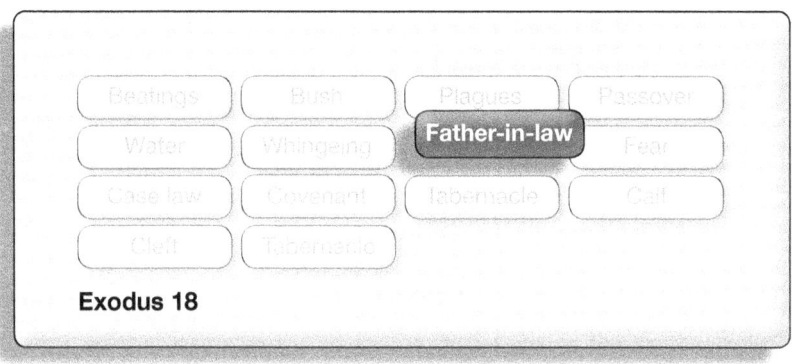

Exodus 18

Now we come to one of our favourite characters in Exodus, namely Moses' father-in-law Jethro. There's nothing in the divinely inspired account that tells us that he has a beard, a checked lumberjack shirt and a 4×4 jeep, but somehow that's the image we can't shake off!

To our shame, Jethro didn't even get a mention in our *original* fourteen-word summary of Exodus. We weren't planning on giving him any more than a paragraph. It's amazing what you learn when you start to dig deeper, and how God humbles you, and how things you didn't understand at first come wonderfully to life. We got Jethro wrong. We underestimated his significance. Now here he is, with a whole chapter all to himself.

Dig Deeper! Structure tool
Where have we met Jethro before? And for that matter his daughter Zippy and grandson Gershom?

> Remember that one of the ways an author marks out a section is to enclose it within a pair of bookends.
>
> What comes in between Jethro/Zippy/Gershom and Jethro/Zippy/Gershom?
>
> Why might the author want us to treat this section as a whole?
>
> Can you identify an overall theme for the section?

The first half of the Jethro story (18:1–12) goes a bit like this. Jethro is watching *BBC News 24* and sees that his son-in-law's God, Yahweh, has pulled off a spectacular rescue. He pings off an email: 'Hey son, Zippy and the kids are desperate to see you. We're coming to visit.' An emotional family reunion follows, and Moses pours out the story of the last seventeen chapters. Jethro is over the moon at how Yahweh had rescued them: 'Now I know that Yahweh is greater than all the other gods, because they thought they could stand up to him, and look what happened!' And Jethro offers sacrifices in praise to God.

So much for our rough summary. But there's much more to be gleaned if we look closely at the details of the text. Read 18:1–12 again, and see what you can find.

Were you reaching for the **Repetition tool** (hint)? The author tells us that Moses had chosen the name Eliezer for his second child because 'the God of my father was my help and *delivered* me' (verse 4). Later, Moses tells Jethro 'how Yahweh had *delivered* them' (verse 8), and Jethro rejoices that Yahweh 'had *delivered* them' and says 'Blessed be Yahweh who has *delivered* you . . . and has *delivered* the people' (verses 9–10). It's kind of hard to miss the emphasis!

Were you reaching for the **Linking Words tool**? Look again at verse 11. Whenever you see a 'therefore', you should always ask what it's *there for*. And the same goes for a 'because'. Jethro confesses Yahweh as the supreme God *because* of the arrogance of the other gods.

Now that's confusing. Who are these 'gods', what did they do that was so arrogant, and how did their arrogance prove them inferior to Yahweh? Most of the commentaries seem to favour what our friend Kyla calls the Skipping Over tool on this verse! Much as we're tempted to do the same, we thought it would make a good case study of what to do with a tricky verse.

First, we reached for the **Translations tool**. Is it just the ESV that's confusing us? Does another translation put it more clearly? Let's compare them:

> Now I know that Yahweh is greater than all gods, because in this affair they dealt arrogantly with the people. (ESV)

> Now I know that Yahweh is greater than all other gods, for he did this to those who had treated Israel arrogantly. (NIV)

> Now I know that Yahweh is greater than all the gods; for in the very thing in which they behaved proudly, He was above them. (NKJV)

> I know now that Yahweh is greater than all other gods, because he rescued his people from the oppression of the proud Egyptians. (NLT)

Everyone is agreed on the first half of the verse! But there are differences of opinion when it comes to the second. What confused us about the ESV was the idea that Yahweh was greater than the gods 'because *they* . . . ' How does their arrogance demonstrate Yahweh's superiority? All of the other translations say that he's greater 'because *he* . . . ' (there are other differences between them, which it would be wise to leave to the Hebrew boffins). If we go with the NIV, NKJV or NLT, then Yahweh is seen to be the greatest because of something *he* did to the 'gods' when they acted in arrogance. That seems to make a bit more sense.

Next we reached for the **Vocabulary tool** to see if we can make sense of the reference to 'gods'. Bible words have Bible meanings, and so we need to look elsewhere in Exodus to see how the author uses this word. The plague on the firstborn was directed 'against all the gods of Egypt' (12:12), and the number-one hit single 'The Horse and His Rider' included the lyrics, 'Who is like you, Yahweh, among the gods?' (15:11). In both of these cases, the 'gods' refer to those things in which the Egyptians put their confidence as rivals to Yahweh, and whom Yahweh soundly defeated. Ancient sources tell us that the Egyptians worshipped the Nile, but Yahweh turned it to blood. They worshipped Min as a fertility god, but it was the Israelites who kept all the midwives busy. The most obvious 'god' in Egypt is Pharaoh himself – certainly he had divine aspirations. But Yahweh strikes his firstborn and drowns his troops. The Egyptian sorcerers whom we met in chapter 7 have genuine supernatural powers when it came to conjuring blood and frogs. But by plague number 3, they were out of the race. Are 'gods' real then? As alternative divinities, no. As pretenders to the throne, yes. But Yahweh won't let them pretend for very long.

We need to start to draw things together. This whole exploration began with the **Linking Words tool**. Jethro has come to know that Yahweh is supreme *because* of the way he dealt with his arrogant rivals in the plagues and at the Red Sea (tricky verse solved!). Combine that with the results of the **Repetition tool**.

Jethro was delighted that Yahweh had delivered and delivered and delivered his people. In summary:

- Jethro confesses that Yahweh saved his people
- Jethro confesses that Yahweh smashed his enemies

This seems a pretty comprehensive summary of the first half of Exodus! Did your use of the **Structure tool** (in the Dig Deeper! exercise) anticipate that?

So what?
So have we arrived at the author's purpose? Was Exodus 18 written *just* to provide us with a neat summary of the story so far? No. The Holy Spirit didn't breathe out these verses purely to consolidate our database of trivia. He wants the truth to affect us somehow, to change us. Time for the **So What? tool** again (together with a little help from the rest of the toolkit).

The **Who am I? tool** asks whom, if anyone, we ought to identify with in the narrative. The **Copycat tool** asks whether, having identified with someone, we should see his behaviour as exemplary, something we should seek to imitate. Often it's important to ask these questions separately, but on this occasion we're going to combine them to create a Whom Should I Copy? tool. There are two options, two possible so whats.

If the author's purpose is for us to copy Moses, then this chapter is an encouragement to evangelism. Throughout Exodus it's clear that God's mighty deeds are not to be kept a secret. God wants them announced to children and grandchildren (10:2), to Joshua (17:14), to 'all the earth' (9:16). Here Moses tells his father-in-law, who happens to be a pagan priest! It's hard enough to talk to your family about the gospel at the best of times, and Jethro would (you'd think) be a particularly hard nut to crack. But as it is, the second he hears Moses' testimony, he's on his knees praising God.

Imagine a re-run of the Moses-Jethro conversation at work on a Monday morning:

'Hey Mose, how's it going? Good weekend?'

'Yeah. Fantastic time. Might sound weird but the best bit was church on Sunday.'

'Oh?'

'You've heard of the parting of the Red Sea, right? Well we were just looking at what actually happened, and it was pretty immense.'

'Good for you. Yes, I guess it's nice to have some kind of spiritual connection, but it's different for different people, isn't it? For you it's Jesus, for Ahmed it's Mohammad, for me . . . I dunno, maybe golf？' [*Jeth smiles, mentally watching the replay of that nine-iron chip out of the rough straight on to the green.*]

'The thing is that God doesn't really tolerate rivals. That's sort of the point in Exodus. Pharaoh tries to set himself up as another god, but the real God defeats him – all the plagues and so on.'

A little later in the conversation . . .
'This is crazy. I never thought I'd say this but . . . what do I have to do to become a Christian?'

Impossible? No. It worked over 3,000 years ago with a priest from Midian. And Yahweh's done the same thing literally millions of times since then. So we dare you. Dare you to leave this book on the desk at work, and when someone asks what you're reading, tell her something about Yahweh, something about how he saves people and smashes his rivals. Who knows, maybe she will do a Jethro?

While this is a helpful line of thought, we ought to be just a *bit* careful about modelling ourselves on Moses the Evangelist. After all, we had little in common with Moses the Talker-to-Burning-Bushes or Moses the Turner-of-Water-to-Blood or Moses the Parter-of-Seas. Moses-is-me assumptions have got our knuckles rapped a couple of times already, and we should tread carefully.

There is another, much safer, answer to the question: whom should I copy? Namely Jethro. After all, Jethro's response to the last seventeen chapters is pretty spot on: Jethro is the very embodiment of the *so what*.

Let's just recap what Jethro does with the news of God's great deeds. He is delighted. He praises God. He confesses that Yahweh is supreme over all rivals. He offers a burnt offering and other sacrifices.

Sacrifices. Did you notice that? At last, someone brings a sacrifice in worship. We've been waiting for this for half the book (**Context tool** alert!). Moses' original request to Pharaoh way back in chapter 5 was to 'let us go a three days' journey into the wilderness that we may sacrifice to Yahweh our God' (5:3). Moses considered sacrifices so important that he even turned down an early offer of freedom because of a shortage of sacrificial animals (10:25). Worshipping Yahweh and offering sacrifices to him was kind of integral to the whole getting-out-of-Egypt project! But so far, God's people have offered no sacrifices, as far as we know. All they've done is whinge.

Along comes Jethro. Within just four verses he seems to get everything right.

Just like the Israelites, *we* have been saved by the blood of a lamb. Like the Israelites, we have seen our enemy defeated. So what? So live a life of whingeing, complaining about the uncomfortable seats in church, the lateness of the number twenty-five bus (autobiographical note here), the tedium of the last few weeks at work? Or . . .

. . . do a Jethro? Praise God. Confess that Yahweh is supreme over all rivals. 'Present your bodies as a living sacrifice, holy and acceptable to God, which is your spiritual worship' (Romans 12:1).

Jethro, the management consultant

Exodus 18:13–27 is a favourite with the corporate gurus. The authors of *Organizational Behavior and Public Management* get pretty excited when Jethro tells Moses 'to delegate, strategically plan and develop an organization design', and according to *The Boundaryless Organization Field Guide* (yes, books like this really do exist), this part of the Bible contains 'one of the earliest instances of management consulting'.

It goes a bit like this. Moses is holding a 24–7 clinic for anyone who wants to know God's will on an issue or needs a dispute resolved. His services are popular, to say the least. The queue reaches to the Red Sea and back, and if you phone the Moses switchboard it gets rerouted to a call centre in Mumbai where they keep you on hold indefinitely. Moses' work-life balance has got out of hand. The doctor is worried about his blood pressure, and Zippy and the kids never get to see him.

Straightaway, Jethro the management consultant (presumably now changed out of lumberjack outfit into pin-striped suit) puts his finger on the issue. 'There's a bottleneck,' he announces, 'inefficiency!' Next thing you know, he's got the laptop out and delivers a polished PowerPoint presentation, gets on the line to the headhunters and appoints several tiers of middle management. Moses keeps his Blackberry switched on in case of an emergency, but the day-to-day running of the country is now in the hands of the new civil service machine.

Much to Zippy's delight, Moses even has time for some DIY around the home.

No doubt there are some useful business tips to be gleaned, but is this *really* the author's purpose? Admittedly, it does seem to be the point in Deuteronomy 1:9–18, where the same situation is described in different words. There the emphasis is on the huge growth of the Israelite population and Moses' inability to cope (**Repetition tool**, verses 9 and 12). But the author's purpose for including this episode in Deuteronomy may not be the same as the reason for including it in Exodus. For example, Jethro doesn't even get a mention in the Deuteronomy account – perhaps because Deuteronomy as a whole is so explicit about the danger of mixing with foreigners when they eventually conquer the Promised Land. In Exodus, on the other hand, Jethro seems pretty key.

The **Context tool** is our best friend in this kind of situation. After all, Exodus 18:13–27 isn't published as a stand-alone pamphlet on management consulting. It belongs with the rest of Exodus, and one feature of the story provides the all-important link to the chapters that follow:

> Moses talking to Jethro: 'when they have a dispute, they come to me and I decide between one person and another, and I make them know the *statutes of God and his laws*' (18:16).

> Jethro talking to Moses: 'you shall warn them about *the statutes and the laws*, and make them know the way in which they must walk and what they must do' (18:20).

You might miss this, except that God's statutes and laws will dominate the second half of the book of Exodus. In *context*, this is the thing that stands out. Moses is overworked – yes, but he is overworked specifically because of the needs of a rescued people to know how God wants them to live. A change is ahead, when God's commandments will no longer come only from the mouth of Moses on a case-by-case basis (as, for example, back in 16:25–30), but will be known much more widely. Jethro's troubleshooting paves the way for tablets of stone (pun intended).

In the first half of chapter 18, we saw that Jethro looks backwards to remind us of God's rescue. In the second half of the chapter, he looks ahead to a people governed by God's statutes and laws. He acts like a giant hinge, holding the two halves of Exodus together! People rescued by God need to live God's way.

Jethro, the foreigner

One little postscript on Jethro's nationality. Having seen Yahweh bash both the Amalekites and the Egyptians, you might be forgiven for thinking he was only interested in the Jews, full stop. So how come Moses is happy to take advice from a Midianite?

Some commentators take this to mean that, as Christians, we should be guided by the teaching of other faiths. That seems rather to miss the point! Jethro has already confessed his faith in Yahweh. He is not offering advice in his capacity as a pagan priest, but as a new convert.

Nonetheless, he is a *Midianite* convert, and this warns us against any notion that the people of God were ever defined purely on the basis of ethnicity. So too does the fact that some of the *Egyptians* were spared from plague 7 because they feared 'the word of Yahweh' (9:20), and that 'a *mixed* multitude also went up' with the Israelites when they left Egypt (12:38), and that in 12:48 directions were given for when a *'stranger'* shares in the Passover meal.

Even in Exodus, there are hints that God would ransom people 'from every tribe and language and people and nation' (Revelation 5:9).

> **BRAINBOX ASIDE: Father-in-law**
>
> We mentioned the **Repetition tool** earlier, when we found 'delivered' appears five times. What we didn't tell you was that it also turned up 'father-in-law' thirteen times! Clearly, the author wants to emphasize that Moses and Jethro are related by marriage. Why? Most of the commentaries use the Skipping Over tool. Can you do better?
>
> Happy digging!

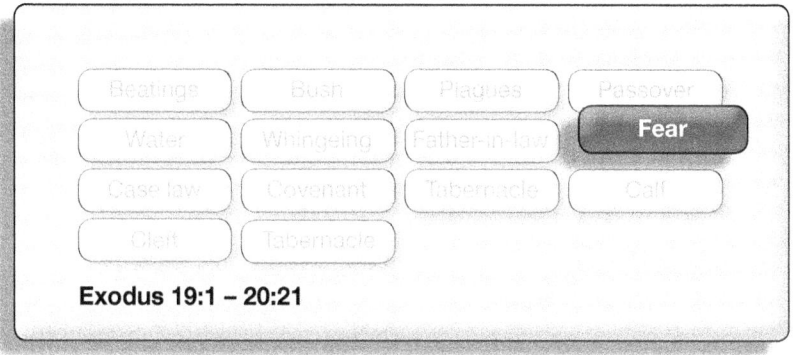

I. You shall have no other gods before me.
II. You shall not make for yourself a carved image.
III. You shall not take the name of Yahweh your God in vain.
IV. Remember the Sabbath day, to keep it holy.
V. Honour your father and your mother.
VI. You shall not murder.
VII. You shall not commit adultery.
VIII. You shall not steal.
IX. You shall not bear false witness.
X. You shall not covet.

Here they are: the Big Ten, the most famous rules in history. They more or less speak for themselves, but we did enjoy one author's attempt to make them more accessible to Da Hood. For example:

VI. You won't snuff out a life, stop someone's clock, blow anyone away, bump anyone off, dole out the big chill, erase, drop, hit, top, waste anyone.
VIII. You won't thieve, nick, lift, blag, fleece, half-inch, swipe or get sticky-fingered.[1]

These are the statutes and laws that God lays down for his people. It's a beautiful way to live, a rock-solid foundation for society. It makes sense to follow the Maker's instructions for life in his world.

But they aren't just the Ten Commandments. They are Exodus chapter twenty, verses three to seventeen! We need to read them as part of Exodus, tasting the Exodus flavours, listening to the Exodus theme tune, wearing our Exodus hats.

Try, for example, reading the third commandment wearing an Exodus hat. See what we mean? There's a lot more to it than trying to avoid bad language, and learning to say 'Oh sugar'. This is about God's *name* and, well, that's pretty much what the whole book of Exodus has been about! Just one commandment opens up a whole world of Exodus truth.

The **Structure tool** is first out of the box, and immediately we find that we have a sandwich on our hands.

A. Events at Mount Sinai: thunder, lightning, smoke and trumpet (19:1–25)
  B. Ten Commandments (20:1–17)
A. Events at Mount Sinai: thunder, lightning, smoke and trumpet (20:18–21)

Clearly there's a connection between Sinai and the statutes, between the Maker's instructions and the mountain. A right understanding of the Ten Commandments will depend on a right understanding of the events at Mount Sinai. Let's pick up the narrative in chapter 19.

Rescued for relationship

> Now therefore, if you will indeed obey my voice and keep my covenant, you shall be my treasured possession among all peoples, for all the earth is mine.
> (19:5)

On first hearing, this sounds as if God's favour has to be earned through good works. The Ten Commandments have become an exam: pass and you're in, fail and you're out. But the **Context tool** kicks that misunderstanding immediately into touch:

> You yourselves have seen what I did to the Egyptians, and how I bore you on eagles' wings and brought you to myself.
> (19:4)

The call to obey God's voice is addressed to people who have already been rescued by eagle. Of course, that's not a literal description of their journey (they walked), but a metaphor for the way in which God guided and protected them. While other modes of transport in the ancient world were fraught with danger – bandits on the road, storms at sea, Egyptian chariots in the desert – those lucky enough to have the Almighty as their Travel Agent are guaranteed safe passage. Eagle-travel is synonymous with loving rescue.

God saved them by his grace alone. But he saved them *for* a relationship. And that relationship requires their obedience.

Exactly the same point is made at the beginning of the Ten Commandments themselves (one of the **Context tool** examples in the original *Dig Deeper*). If we start with 'No gods before me', then it sounds like nothing more than a list of rules to be kept. But Exodus 20 doesn't start that way. It starts with what we call the zeroth commandment:

> And God spoke all these words, saying, 'I am Yahweh your God, who brought you out of the land of Egypt, out of the house of slavery.'
> (20:1–2)

God isn't asking them to worship their way into his good books, any more than they worshipped their way out of Egypt. He saved them by his grace alone. But he saved them *for* a relationship. And that relationship requires their obedience.

Linking Words tool
How has the rest of Exodus prepared us for this scene atop Mount Sinai? What is the connection between rescue and obedient service in 7:16; 8:1, 20; 9:1, 13; 10:3?

Most relationships, when you come to think about it, are governed by certain rules. It's expected in a marriage that you don't sleep with someone else. It's expected in a friendship that you take account of the other person's likes and dislikes and don't go out of your way to upset them. That's one of the reasons why the start of a friendship can be a bit awkward: you don't yet know the person well enough to avoid putting your foot in it; you don't know what the unwritten rules *are*.

Wanting to avoid such awkwardness, Andrew tells Richard a little about himself early in their friendship. He loves Beethoven but draws the line at death metal; he finds a glass of vintage port a real treat but turns up his nose at malt whisky. He loves the BBC drama *Spooks*, but would sooner read a book than watch Formula One. Richard secretly auctions Andrew's *Spooks* DVD box set on Ebay, and uses the money to buy the latest album by the American band, Knights of the Abyss. This he presents to Andrew for Christmas, together with a bottle of Glenmorangie Single Malt and tickets for Silverstone. Being English, Andrew politely thanks Richard, and even manages a weak smile. But their friendship is on the line.

Mount Sinai, in some ways, is the beginning of a friendship with Yahweh. He's rescued them, and wants them to be his 'treasured possession'. But if the relationship is to be close and intimate, they need to know his character, his likes and dislikes. It turns out that God isn't too fussed about different types of music (he listens to organs and Christian youth rock bands with equal pleasure!), but he draws the line at worship of other gods and idolatry. He says nothing of his favourite tipple, but turns his nose up at murder and adultery. He doesn't want a box set of *Spooks* for Christmas, but he loves it when children honour their parents, and witnesses tell the truth in court. To disregard utterly his Commandments is to ignore his character and put the friendship on the line.

On the eve of his crucifixion, Jesus said, 'If you love me, you will keep my commandments' (John 14:15). Obviously he's not giving his disciples a ladder to climb to reach heaven. He's come down from heaven to die to get them there, an eagles'-wings deliverance, if ever there was one. But he saved them *for* a relationship. And that relationship requires their obedience. That's why when we turn to the New Testament we find that the principles expressed in the original Big Ten are restated for the church.

(As an aside: Christians differ as to whether the Sabbath commandment remains in force today, since it is not explicitly restated in the New Testament, but all agree that the intention behind this commandment is to point to the perfect heavenly 'rest' for which we have been rescued: see Hebrews 4:1–10.)

So What? tool

Consider each of the commandments in turn. What will a loving relationship with Jesus look like in your life this week? Be as specific as you can.

I	VI
II	VII
III	VIII
IV	IX
V	X

In the Sermon on the Mount (it's no accident that Jesus gave his most famous sermon atop a mountain!), Jesus took some of the Ten Commandments and applied them more radically. Hatred can lead to murder. Lust can lead to adultery. As rescued members of his kingdom, look over the Commandments again, thinking now not only of your outward actions but of the secrets of your heart.

As further reading on these things, we'd highly recommend John Frame's mammoth (but very accessible) volume, *The Doctrine of the Christian Life* (P. & R. Publishing).

When God puts the fear of God into you

Just to remind you where we've got to, we established using the **Structure tool** that a right understanding of the Ten Commandments depends on a right understanding of the goings-on at Mount Sinai. And one of the things you can't miss about the Mount Sinai narrative is the emphasis on fear.

The Bible talks a lot about the fear of the Lord. You'll find it especially often in Psalms and Proverbs, but also on the lips of Jesus (e.g. Luke 12:5) and the apostles (e.g. Revelation 14:7). It's there in our passage in Exodus 20:20. Using the **Vocabulary tool**, we have to ask: what does that phrase actually *mean*?

Does it mean that we should simply 'respect' or 'revere' God (sometimes the phrase is translated that way)? Has the Christian surfer dude got it right when he says that God is 'awesome' (sometimes it gets translated that way too)? Or is it a bit stronger than that? Is it actually about being scared of God?

Being scared of things isn't something we normally aspire to. Indeed, one of the Bible words for fear is *phobos*, from which we get the English word 'phobia'. Phobias aren't to be cultivated by well-adjusted people!

(Note to boffins: strictly speaking it's a logical fallacy to read modern connotations of a word back into its ancient meaning. When Paul wrote about *dynamis* ['power'] he wasn't thinking about dynamite, because it wasn't going to be invented for another 2,000 years! And when Peter wrote of *phobos*, he wasn't thinking of twenty-first-century psychology. We're using the analogy for illustration purposes only. Humour us.)

Thanks to the wonders of Google, we came across a list of possible phobias. Our favourites ones were Ablutophobia (the fear of washing) and Clinophobia (fear of going to bed), both of which we experienced as teenage boys, and Arachibutyrophobia (the fear of peanut butter sticking to the roof of your mouth), which Andrew realizes he still suffers from. Crunchy is safer than smooth, he feels. So how about Theophobia, the fear of God? Surely it would be irrational to fear the God who led you out of Egypt 'in . . . steadfast love' (15:13). He cares about you! He plans to prosper and not to harm you! He's 'Abba', Father. Surely there's no need for your knees to knock?

So when 20:20 talks about the 'fear of him', what kind of fear is it? That's our **Vocabulary tool** project, and because Bible words have Bible meanings, we need to look at how the word is used in these chapters. However strange it might seem, we can't escape the conclusion that the Israelites were badly shaken by their encounter with the Almighty.

First, the preparations are frightening (19:10–15). Yahweh is about to 'come down on Mount Sinai in the sight of all the people', and that necessitates the erection of safety barriers around the perimeter. Anyone who crosses the barrier and touches the mountain has to be put to death immediately by stone or arrow, presumably so that the executioner remains at a safe distance and avoids touching the mountain himself. These aren't the kind of instructions you'd get at a village fête: 'Don't touch the tombola or you'll die.' It's deliberately unsettling.

Secondly, the third day itself is frightening. Both the mountain and the people tremble:

> On the morning of the third day there were thunders and lightnings and a thick cloud on the mountain and a very loud trumpet blast, so that all the people in the camp trembled. Then Moses brought the people out of the camp to meet God, and they took their stand at the foot of the mountain. Now Mount Sinai was wrapped in smoke because Yahweh had descended on it in fire. The smoke of it went up like the smoke of a kiln, and the whole mountain trembled greatly. And as the sound of the trumpet grew louder and louder,

Moses spoke, and God answered him in thunder. Yahweh came down on Mount Sinai, to the top of the mountain. And Yahweh called Moses to the top of the mountain, and Moses went up. (19:16–20)

Thirdly, the reminder is frightening. Having already set safety limits around the mountain, Moses is urged to hurry back down the mountain and warn the people again not to 'break through to Yahweh to look and many of them perish' (19:21). The instruction hardly seems necessary – the people are way too scared at this point to come anywhere near! Nonetheless, God repeats the warning for a *third time*: 'Do not let the priests and the people break through to come up to Yahweh, lest he break out against them' (19:24).

Finally, the response is that of a frightened people (20:18–21): 'You speak to us, and we will listen,' they say to Moses, 'but do not let God speak to us, lest we die.' They stand 'far off' and tremble in their boots, rightly conscious of their need for a mediator. This is the context in which Moses refers to the 'fear' of Yahweh. 'Respect' or 'reverence' don't really capture the meaning adequately. 'Terrified' would be closer. And it seems to be quite deliberate on God's part. God has put the fear of God into them.

But we're not quite ready to put the **Vocabulary tool** back into its box, because 20:20 contains a play on words:

> Moses said to the people, '*Do not fear*, for God has come to test you, that the *fear of him* may be before you, that you may not sin.'

Don't be afraid, but do fear God. That's what Moses seems to be saying. Don't conclude from the loud trumpet and the smoke and the safety limits that God is out to get to you. Don't be so scared that you don't want him to speak to you. He's a good God and he's on your side. He rescued you by eagle, remember. He wants you as his treasured possession. But there is a *healthy* fear of him; there is a safe distance at which to stand (not 'far off' maybe, but neither waltzing up to the mountain to touch it willy-nilly); there is an attitude to God that will make you think twice before sinning against him.

Fear of that kind, the 'think-twice-before-you-sin' fear, frames the Ten Commandments. You keep your eyes off the other woman because of your love for your own wife (hopefully), but also in part because you are scared of what God would think. You look after your ageing parents because you genuinely care about them (hopefully), but also in part because it would be terrifying to face God on judgment day and have to explain to him why you hadn't bothered.

Context tool

This isn't the first time the idea of fear has cropped up in Exodus. How does the wider context of Exodus add to your understanding of what it means to 'fear him'?

Look at 1:15–21. How is fear of God shown in action?

Look at 9:18–21. How is fear of God shown in action? Why was the fear appropriate, given what happened next?

Does 'think-twice-before-you-sin' fear still apply to us today? That's a **Bible Timeline tool** question, and we ought always to ask it when reading the Old Testament. Has anything changed this side of Jesus? We don't paint our doorposts with

Passover blood any more. God doesn't promise to deal with your oppressive boss the way he did with Pharaoh. Ought we still to fear him?

Some would instinctively say 'no', perhaps citing 1 John 4:18: 'Perfect love casts out fear.' But which fear does perfect love drive out? Moses himself disapproved of one kind of fear while commending another.

OK, some say, what about Hebrews 12:18–29? There the writer tells his Christian readers that they have '*not come* to what may be touched, a blazing fire and darkness and gloom and a tempest and the sound of a trumpet and a voice whose words made the hearers beg that no further messages be spoken to them'. So there's no need to be afraid like poor old Moses and the Israelites were.

We need to take care with these verses. The writer to the Hebrews is comparing Mount Sinai in the Old Testament with Mount Zion in the New, and it's true that in many ways Zion comes out on top. But is non-scariness one of Zion's trump cards? Is it better because it's less frightening? Actually no. Using the **Quotation/Allusion tool** you can't help but notice that the writer deliberately employs the *scariest* of the available Sinai imagery to describe Zion. If anything, we are to fear God more, not less.

Sinai (life as an Old Testament Israelite)	Zion (life as a Christian)
'Yahweh had descended . . . in fire' (Exodus 19:18).	'Our God is a consuming fire' (Hebrews 12:29).
'The whole mountain trembled greatly' (Exodus 19:18).	'Yet once more I will shake not only the earth but also the heavens' (Hebrews 12:26).

Sinai (life as an Old Testament Israelite)	Zion (life as a Christian)
Rejecting God's commandments is a serious matter (e.g. Exodus 20:5).	Rejecting God's words now is even more serious than rejecting what he said through Moses (Hebrews 12:25).
'The fear of him may be before you, that you may not sin' (Exodus 20:20).	'Let us offer to God acceptable worship, with reverence and awe' (Hebrews 12:28).

Nothing changes, fear-wise, as we move from Moses to Christ. Indeed, the very same 'don't-be-afraid-but-fear-God formula' that we discovered in Exodus 20:20 resurfaces on the lips of Jesus:

> I tell you, my friends, do not fear those who kill the body, and after that have nothing more that they can do. But I will warn you whom to fear: fear him who, after he has killed, has authority to cast into hell. Yes, I tell you, fear him! Are not five sparrows sold for two pennies? And not one of them is forgotten before God. Why, even the hairs of your head are all numbered. Fear not; you are of more value than many sparrows.
> (Luke 12:4–7)

In *The Lion, the Witch and the Wardrobe*, C. S. Lewis brilliantly captures what it means to fear someone who is good, with no conflict between trembling and loving intimacy. It comes just after Mr Beaver tells the children that Aslan (the Christ figure in the book) is a lion:

'Ooh!' said Susan, 'I'd thought he was a man. Is he – quite safe? I shall feel rather nervous about meeting a lion.'

'That you will, dearie, and no mistake,' said Mrs Beaver. 'If there is anyone who can appear before Aslan without their knees knocking, they're either braver than most or else just plain silly.'

'Then he isn't safe?' said Lucy.

'Safe?' said Mr Beaver, 'don't you know what Mrs Beaver tells you? Who said anything about safe?

'Course he isn't safe. But he's good. He's the King I tell you.'²

So What? tool

What place does the fear of the Lord have in your Christian life?

How (paradoxically) might it help you to grow closer to God?

How might it help you to live in obedience to him as an eagle-rescued person?

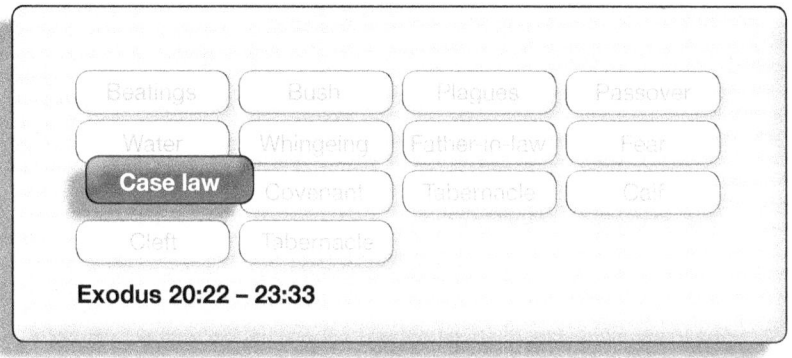

Did you know that it's illegal to wear a suit of armour in Parliament? That eating a mince pie on Christmas Day is forbidden? And placing a postage stamp bearing an image of the Queen's head upside down could be regarded as treason?[1] To our ears, these archaic laws sound bizarre, even humorous, but in their original context they would have made perfect sense. Not a bad idea to ban armour at a time when MPs were apt to settle disputes by duelling! Admittedly, it's harder to see the harm in a mince pie.

What do you make of the biblical prohibition of boiling a young goat in its mother's milk (Exodus 23:19)? It's easy to dismiss some aspects of British law as outdated and irrelevant, but we're nervous about doing the same with the God-given words of Scripture, particularly when Jesus warned that 'not an iota, not a dot, will pass from the Law until all is accomplished' (Matthew 5:18).

The **Genre tool** helps us get our bearings: we have moved

out of the realm of historical narrative and are now dealing with case law.[2] The list seems a bit miscellaneous – what to do when someone knocks out a servant's teeth, then cases of ox-goring, then details of compensation payable by someone who leaves a pit uncovered and a donkey falls into it (21:26–34)! But the same jumbled-up agenda is exactly what you would find in a modern-day magistrates' court: someone who didn't pay their council tax, then a case of domestic violence, then a bunch of students who spray-painted a moustache onto the statue of the vice-chancellor. While the Ten Commandments give the foundational principles, these chapters apply them to a range of practical scenarios as and when they arise. That's how case law works. It's exactly what Jethro was looking for (**Context tool** flashback to 18:13–27) when he suggested that, rather than consult Moses in every situation, it would be better if God's laws and statutes were made widely known.

The thing about case law is that it's inevitably specific to a particular time and place. When we were children, airports imposed no restrictions on carrying fluids in your hand luggage. At the time of writing, you're only allowed bottles of under 100ml because of fears about liquid bombs. It's not that morality has changed, it's just that new situations require new judgments. For these reasons alone, it would be silly simply to transfer the laws of the second millennium BC on to today's statute book. But there are theological considerations also: we do not live 'under the law' in the way that the Israelites did (more on that when we get to Exodus 24).

Having said this, we'd be wrong to dismiss case law as irrelevant to moral judgments today. Paul appeals to it, for example, to support his assertion that Christian leaders must be properly paid:

> Let the elders who rule well be considered worthy of double honour, especially those who labour in preaching and teaching. For the Scripture says, 'You shall not muzzle an ox when it treads out the grain', and, 'The labourer deserves his wages.'
>
> (1 Timothy 5:17–18; see also 1 Corinthians 9:8–10)

The **Linking Words tool** unpacks the 'for': Paul's instruction to honour faithful church leaders is based on what 'the Scripture says'. The **Quotation/Allusion tool** takes us back to Deuteronomy 25:4, and when we dutifully examine the context, we discover that the Scripture in question comes from a collection of case laws very like the one in Exodus. Now it's our guess that if you were reading through Deuteronomy, you might easily dismiss 25:4 as irrelevant. You're probably not a farmer, and even if you are, you presumably process your cereals using a machine, although 'Ox-stampeded Bran Flakes' may well have a place in today's organic food market! But Paul reads Deuteronomy and discerns an underlying *principle* relevant to non-farmers for all time.

And when Jesus teaches that a charge against a fellow Christian must be 'established by the evidence of two or three witnesses' (Matthew 18:16), practitioners of the **Quotation/Allusion tool** will pounce on the reference to Deuteronomy 19:15. Again, a principle from the Old Testament case law is taken and applied to New Testament believers.

As we work through some of the major themes of Exodus 20:22 – 23:33 then, we need to steer a course between two extremes. On the one hand, we ought not to assume that *everything* applies to us exactly as it did to them. We are going to need to keep using the **Bible Timeline tool** lest we take unbiblical shortcuts that bypass Jesus. On the other hand, we ought not to assume that *nothing* applies to us as it did to them – '*All* Scripture is . . . profitable' (2 Timothy 3:16).

Idols and altars, festivals and offerings

Using the **Structure tool**, we noticed that the first block of material (20:22–26) is about worship: no silver gods, no nudity in the tabernacle. And the last block of material (23:14–19) is about worship too: religious feasts and offerings. In between are lots of practical regulations about everyday life. If the structure tells us anything, it is that the sacred and the secular are not to be divorced: Yahweh cares just as much about what goes on at work Monday to Friday as what happens at church on Sunday (or the tabernacle on Saturday).

Slavery

The next issue to be addressed is slavery, and the first few words stick in the throat: 'When you buy a Hebrew slave . . . ' (21:2). Most Christians are embarrassed to find this in the Bible, and are half-tempted to reach for a marker pen and cross these verses out.

But we need *never* be embarrassed about the Bible. We should always find fault with our own feeble understanding before we find fault with words that come from the mouth of God. And so it is here. Maybe we failed to understand it right. Maybe we need to pray, and then dig deeper!

Let's begin with the **Copycat tool**: does the fact that the Bible *describes* slavery mean that it also *prescribes* it? Does biblical law commend every practice it seeks to regulate? Obviously not. This was the Pharisees' mistake when they read the case law about divorce. They assumed that just because Moses gave a ruling about it, it must be OK in God's eyes. But Jesus explained, 'Because of your hardness of heart he wrote you this commandment' (Mark 10:5). In other words, the divorce law exists not because God is pro-divorce but because we share the same coronary diagnosis as Pharaoh.

The same is true of slavery. Elsewhere in the Old Testament it's clear that to enslave a fellow Israelite is absolutely wrong, and for a reason that readers of Exodus should hardly need to have spelled out for them:

> If your brother becomes poor beside you and sells himself to you, you shall not make him serve as a slave . . . For they are my servants, whom I brought out of the land of Egypt; they shall not be sold as slaves.
> (Leviticus 25:39, 42, with thanks to the **Linking Words tool**)

It would be more than a little ironic to be delivered from slavery to Pharaoh, only to find yourself enslaved to a fellow Israelite. Ironic maybe. But not inconceivable. Such are the hard hearts of the rescued Israelites that that they need laws to regulate (not to approve but to regulate) slavery when it happens.

When we read the case law of Exodus with all of this in mind, we discover that God's concern is primarily for the *protection* of slaves: every slave automatically receives his freedom after seven years (21:2) along with his wife (verse 3). A slave-girl cannot be sold to foreigners (verse 8); if she marries the son of an Israelite, she is given the status of a daughter (verse 9). If a slave is beaten to death, his master will face justice (verse 20); if the slave is harmed in some other way, the slave must be set free and compensated (verses 26–27).

Thanks to God's laws, the treatment of slaves in Israel was a million miles away from the brutality seen on the West-Indian sugar and coffee plantations from the sixteenth until the nineteenth century. Verse 5 even envisages the possibility that a slave might decline the offer of freedom, preferring to remain in the household of a master he has come to love.

But to restate the point: Exodus is not saying slavery is a good thing.

Criminal justice
One of Andrew's friends is doing his pupillage as a barrister and owns a copy of *Archbold*, a monstrously thick volume that tells you how much you can expect to be punished for breaking each of the laws currently in force in the United Kingdom. It's fun to try to guess the prison term for a particular misdemeanour and then look it up to see if you got it right (at least Andrew thinks this is fun).

The next block of case laws outline, Archbold-style, the penalties due for different crimes. For example:

> When men strive together and hit a pregnant woman, so that her children come out, but there is no harm, the one who hit her shall surely be fined, as the woman's husband shall impose on him, and he shall pay as the judges determine. But if there is harm, then you shall pay life for life, eye for eye, tooth for tooth, hand for hand, foot for foot, burn for burn, wound for wound, stripe for stripe.
> (21:22–25)

> When an ox gores a man or a woman to death, the ox shall be stoned, and its flesh shall not be eaten, but the owner of the ox shall not be liable. But if the ox has been accustomed to gore in the past, and its owner has been warned but has not kept it in, and it kills a man or a woman, the ox shall be stoned, and its owner also shall be put to death.
> (21:28–29)[3]

If a man steals an ox or a sheep, and kills it or sells it, he shall repay five oxen for an ox, and four sheep for a sheep.
(22:1)

There are a few principles worth drawing out. Notice first that justice requires compensation for the injured party (e.g. 'five oxen for an ox') and punishment for the offender (e.g. 'shall be put to death'). To slip into preacher-mode and use two words beginning with the same letter, it's about restitution and retribution. This contrasts starkly with some modern penal theory that focuses exclusively on (a third 'r') rehabilitating the offender. C. S. Lewis explores the consequences of ditching the biblical position in his little essay 📖 'The Humanitarian Theory of Punishment', something that every Christian should read (it's free online).[4]

Notice secondly that the sentencing must be proportionate: 'life for life, eye for eye, tooth for tooth'[5] – or in the immortal words of Gilbert and Sullivan:

> My object all sublime
> I shall achieve in time –
> To let the punishment fit the crime –
> The punishment fit the crime.

Notice thirdly that the punishment must take account of the extent to which the defendant was culpable for what went wrong: 'if the ox has been accustomed to gore in the past . . . ' In modern legal terminology, this amounts to the requirement of a *mens rea*, a mental component to the crime (why do lawyers love Latin so much?). A toy manufacturer whose 'My First Salon' hairdryer unexpectedly overheats causing a house fire (despite rigorous safety testing) would not be liable, but one who bought a job lot of military-surplus flamethrowers on the cheap and repackaged them to flog as toy hairdryers for the Christmas market . . .

Before we rush to apply these lessons to today, we need to use the **Bible Timeline tool** and ask whether anything has changed this side of the coming of Jesus. Actually, for all of the developments in the history of salvation, the one thing that *hasn't* altered is the moral fabric of the universe. That is because true ethics and true justice are grounded in the character of God, and with him 'there is no variation or shadow due to change' (James 1:17).

Thus, even if we don't want to go the whole way with the theonomists (those Christians who want to see the civil laws of the Bible adopted as the blueprint for modern society), we can be grateful that some of the principles enshrined in Exodus have found their way into British law. This heritage is under attack from secularists, and we must play our part in defending it.[6]

But the laws in Exodus tell us much more than the kind of justice we might hope to establish in contemporary society. They tell us of the kind of justice we can expect on the day when the Son of Man sits on his judgment throne and all the nations gather together before him. There we will see retribution, proportionate sentencing, and assessment of culpability, perfectly combined: 'He will render to each one according to his works' (Romans 2:6).

Social justice
As we were reading through these chapters, the **Repetition tool** highlighted an injunction that comes twice:

> You shall not wrong a sojourner or oppress him, for you were sojourners in the land of Egypt.
> (22:21)

> You shall not oppress a sojourner. You know the heart of a sojourner, for you were sojourners in the land of Egypt.
> (23:9)

We wondered, **Structure tool** in hand, whether the author intended these as a pair of bookends to mark out a mini-section. In between these references to the 'sojourner', we get a mention of the 'widow', the 'fatherless' and the 'poor' (three times). Clearly God has a special concern for the vulnerable in society.

One more look at the bookends, and we're reaching for the **Linking Words tool**:

> Don't wrong a sojourner ←for you yourselves were sojourners in Egypt.

Or to flip it around the other way and exchange the 'for' for a 'therefore' (a classic trick of the **Linking Words tool** that can sometimes make the logical connection more obvious):

> You were sojourners in Egypt, →therefore don't wrong a sojourner.

The Israelites' concern for the weak ought to flow naturally from God's care for *them* when *they* were weak. It's a principle found often in Scripture. As the recipients of mercy, we should be quick to dispense mercy; having been forgiven, we should be quick to forgive; having experienced the love of God, we ought to love one another (e.g. Luke 6:36; Ephesians 4:32; 1 John 4:11).

As we've been pondering this chapter, we've come to love the nuances of biblical law. Look at what we found using the **Parallels tool**:

Nor shall you be partial to a poor man in his lawsuit.
(23:3)

You shall not pervert the justice due to your poor in his lawsuit.
(23:6)

The poor man should not be disfavoured in a court of law. Our liberal society feels that strongly – we are outraged when the supermarket chain tramples the small-time supplier, or the multinational oil corporation puts a low price on the lives of Nigerian villagers – and the Bible agrees. But neither should the poor man be unjustly *favoured*. How surprising that the Bible includes that! How perceptive to see that poverty is no guarantee of innocence, that one could be a victim and yet a sinner at the same time. How perfectly, beautifully just to demand of the law courts that the poor get treated not better, nor worse, but the *same*.

Clearly social justice is a huge priority in Exodus. But before we rush to draw lessons for today, we need to use the **Bible Timeline tool** and ask whether anything has changed this side of the coming of Jesus. And something has, as we've tried to show in this little diagram:

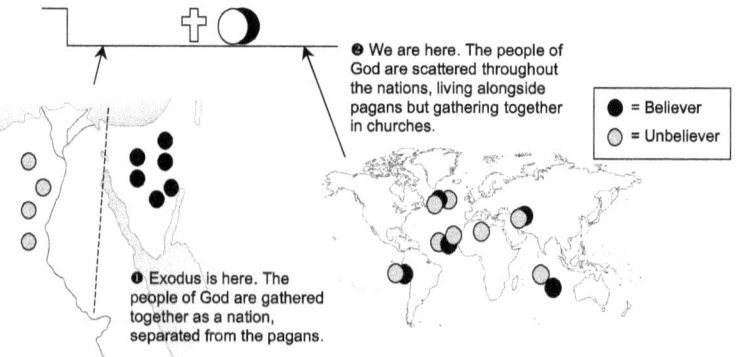

Figure 2

At Sinai, the people of God are gathered together as a nation. Together they had been rescued from Egypt; together they are travelling toward the Promised Land; together they are governed by God's statutes and laws. When God tells them to look out for the poor and oppressed, he is referring to the poor fellow-Israelite, the oppressed kinsman.

It should be obvious that the modern-day equivalent of Israel is not the United Kingdom but the church. Accordingly, these passages from Exodus don't speak primarily to the issue of helping the poor in society at large. Rather, they apply to relationships between *Christians*, both locally (within your church family) and globally (with brothers and sisters from across the world). That is why, when we get to the New Testament, we find that the emphasis is on doing good to the poor or widow or orphan within the Christian community:

> There was not a needy person among them [i.e. among the Christians], for as many as were owners of lands or houses sold them and brought the proceeds of what was sold and laid it at the apostles' feet, and it was distributed to each as any had need.
> (Acts 4:34–35)

> At present, however, I am going to Jerusalem bringing aid to the saints [i.e. Christians]. For Macedonia and Achaia have been pleased to make some contribution for the poor among the saints at Jerusalem.
> (Romans 15:25–26)

> So then, as we have opportunity, let us do good to everyone, and especially to those who are of the household of faith [i.e. Christians].
> (Galatians 6:10)

> Honour widows who are truly widows . . . She who is truly a
> widow, left all alone, has set her hope on God [i.e. she is a Christian]
> and continues in supplications and prayers night and day.
> (1 Timothy 5:3, 5)

> Religion that is pure and undefiled before God, the Father, is this:
> to visit orphans and widows in their affliction . . . Listen, my beloved
> brothers, has not God chosen those who are poor in the world to be
> rich in faith and heirs of the kingdom, which he has promised to
> those who love him? [i.e. we're talking about Christians].
> (James 1:27; 2:5)

> If a brother or sister [i.e. a Christian] is poorly clothed and lacking
> in daily food, and one of you says to them, 'Go in peace, be
> warmed and filled,' without giving them the things needed for the
> body, what good is that?
> (James 2:15–16)

Without wanting to be controversialists, we need to mention that a couple of recent evangelical books on the subject of social justice have not been as careful as they might have been with the **Bible Timeline tool.** They point out, rightly, what a huge theme social justice is in the Old Testament, but from this they derive a mandate for the church to set up soup kitchens and homeless shelters for the destitute in society at large. At worst, this threatens to eclipse the church's priority of proclaiming the message of the gospel. We need to get back to the pattern of the early church in the book of Acts: *within the Christian community* there was a great concern for the poor, but when it came to those outside, their supreme concern was for the lost.

We're not saying that Christians are wrong to show compassion for the needy outside the church – we really meant it when we sang the praises of Lord Shaftesbury and William Wilberforce a few chapters back, and Galatians 6:10 commends it (notwithstanding the 'especially'). We're just saying that this is an area where we need to take care in our handling of the Bible, and where care has not always been taken.

In summary, the 'social' laws of Exodus speak first and foremost to our dealings with vulnerable Christians. And here it really bites. When we read of the aftermath of the war in Iraq, how quickly do our thoughts turn to the *church* there? When Oxfam launches an appeal to help victims of an earthquake in Haiti, do we think of sending aid specifically to brothers and sisters? Or closer to home, is it only the middle-class people at church, with BUPA health insurance, who can get the hip operation they need? Or will the cell group stump up a couple of grand each? How many spare rooms does the homeless person in the congregation have to choose from? The church ought to be the ultimate welfare organization.

On the way to the Promised Land

The Promised Land has been in view from the very beginning of Exodus. God spoke from the burning bush of bringing the Israelites to 'a land flowing with milk and honey, to the place of the Canaanites, the Hittites, the Amorites, the Perizzites, the Hivites, and the Jebusites' (3:8; cf. 3:17). A little later on the Israelites sang, accompanied by Miriam on her tambourine, of the terror that would seize the leaders of Edom, Moab and Philistia, as Yahweh guaranteed them safe passage on their journey to the place of Yahweh's dwelling (15:13–18). These are well-worn themes. Why though does the author reintroduce them as he draws his section to an end (23:20–33)?

If we were wanting to sound all theological, we'd say that these final paragraphs introduce the 'eschatological dimension'.

Eschatology is just a posh term for living in the present in the light of the future.

Having spotted the eschatological perspective here in chapter 23, it dawned on us that we'd actually seen it already back in the Ten Commandments themselves:

> Honour your father and your mother, that your days may be long in the land that Yahweh your God is giving you.
> (20:12, with thanks again to the **Linking Words tool**)

OK, so one of the motives for the Israelites to keep God's commandments in the desert is the prospect of living one day in the land. Does that still apply to us? Yes! We got pretty excited when, using the **Quotation/Allusion tool**, we remembered what Paul says to New Testament believers in Ephesians 6:2–3:

> 'Honour your father and mother' (this is the first commandment with a promise), 'that it may go well with you and that you may live long in the land.'
> (Ephesians 6:2–3)

It's significant that Paul restates for the Christian church, not only the Exodus instruction but also the Exodus motivation. We too are awaiting the Promised Land. And that ought to shape our life here in the desert. We should start living *now* the way that we will live forever (see Colossians 3:1–2). To summarize it all, a final **Bible Timeline tool** diagram is shown in Figure 3 on the next page.

Before we finish, there was just one other detail in chapter 23 that we couldn't pass over. As we read it, the lights on our **Author's Purpose tool** started to flash, and we began to hear

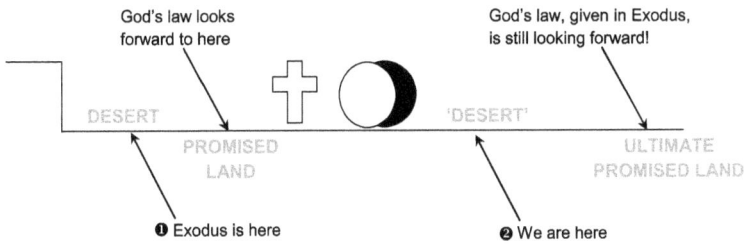

Figure 3

the familiar melody of the Exodus theme tune. Read 23:20–21 to see if you have the same experience.

How can you be confident of safe passage to the Promised Land? Why ought you to take care to obey God on the way? Because of the angel of whom God says, 'My name is in him.' Which name would that be? Yahweh, of course. Sooner or later everything in Exodus comes back to Yahweh and his name.

> **BRAINBOX ASIDE: Instructions for boiling goats**
>
> 'You shall not boil a young goat in its mother's milk' (23:19). Using the **Bible Timeline tool** and others, work out what this has to say to us today.
>
> Happy Digging!

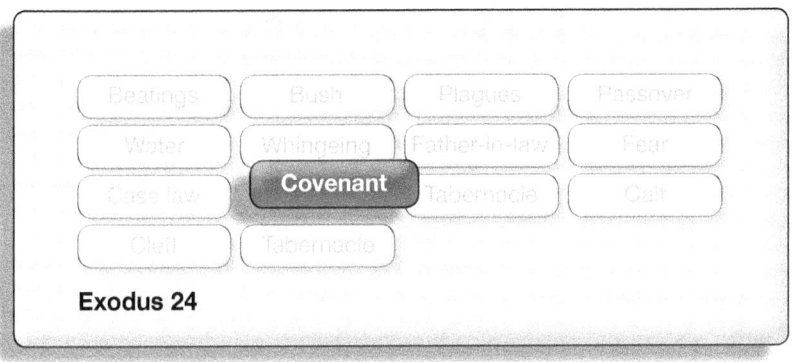

Exodus 24

'Antelopes and albatrosses are apathetic and aren't angry about anything, although an antelope's abhorrent antisocial actions *almost* annoyed an ageing albatross.'

Everyone knows that Christian preachers like words that begin with the same letter, and so here is a chapter all about Covenant, Conditions, Consecration and en-Counter. Yup, even better when there's a really forced one at the end :-)

Covenant

Beginning with the **Structure tool**, we observe that Exodus 19:7–8 and 24:3 act like a huge pair of bookends, marking off a major section:

> So Moses came and called the elders of the people and set before them all these words that Yahweh had commanded him. All the people answered together and said, 'All that Yahweh has spoken we will do.' (19:7–8)

> Moses came and told the people all the words of Yahweh and all the rules. And all the people answered with one voice and said, 'All the words that Yahweh has spoken we will do.'
> (24:3)

Sandwiched in-between come the Ten Commandments (described as 'words', 20:1) and the detailed case laws (described as 'rules', 21:1) that outline how the people are to live in relationship with Yahweh. When 24:3 mentions 'all the words . . . and all the rules' in one breath, we know the author is gathering everything together to a climax: God's covenant relationship with his people is about to be signed and sealed.

Conditions

Next up is the **Repetition tool**: Moses told the people 'all' the words and 'all' the rules (verse 3). He writes 'all' of them down (verse 4) and refers again to 'all' of them (verse 8). The people respond by promising twice that they will obey 'all' that Yahweh said (verses 3, 7).

Anyone who knows the sinfulness of the human heart (or anyone who has read to the end of Exodus!) will be wary of their optimism. What, you're going to get *everything* right? Confident nods. No mistakes at all? Vigorous shakings of the head.

The frightening thing is that their optimism gets bound into the terms of the covenant (verse 8). It's like promising your mortgage company that you won't set off the smoke alarm even once during the twenty-five-year repayment period, and writing it into the contract before you sign. Then, before you've even unpacked all the boxes, you're frying some sausages and . . . Eee-eee-eee-eee. They should have said, 'Yahweh, we're not up to this; you know how much we grumbled in the desert just because we were a little bit thirsty. Please have mercy on us and relax the terms.' But instead they're like, 'Pass the pen so we can sign.'

The whole arrangement is nail-bitingly precarious from the start.

Consecration

As they sign, Moses begins to shower the congregation with blood. When we first read this we were visualizing a scene of Quentin Tarantino-style gore, with jets of blood hitting people square-on in the face, but that's not quite warranted by the text! To understand the imagery of sprinkled blood, we need to look not to Hollywood but to the **Context tool**, and turning over a couple of pages to 29:19–21, we find a similar ritual associated with *consecration to the priesthood*. This link is strengthened by the mention of Aaron and his sons (the priestly family who take centre stage in the later passage) on either side of the covenant ratification (24:1, 9). The interesting thing in chapter 24 is that *everyone* is showered with blood, not the priests only. Perhaps the author's purpose is to show us that all Israel is set apart for service of Yahweh. Notwithstanding Aaron's special role, they are a 'kingdom of priests and a holy nation' (19:6). This important truth is often referred to as 'the priesthood of all believers'. Dog collars all round!

En-counter

After the people have made their rash promises of obedience, and after Moses has sprinkled everyone with blood, a special delegation is allowed for the first time to accompany Moses up the mountain for an encounter with Yahweh:

> Then Moses and Aaron, Nadab, and Abihu, and seventy of the elders of Israel went up, and they saw the God of Israel. There was

under his feet as it were a pavement of sapphire stone, like the very heaven for clearness. And he did not lay his hand on the chief men of the people of Israel; they beheld God, and ate and drank. (24:9–11)

Here is a moment of astonishing intimacy. We've seen already that rules are all about relationship, and here seventy representatives of the people (those appointed as deputies at Jethro's suggestion?) sit down at God's banqueting table for a meal with the Almighty. Presumably the oxen previously sacrificed were on the menu – it was usual for the meat of the offering to become the priests' dinner (e.g. 29:32–33). But the narrative doesn't focus on the food. The amazing thing about this meal is that they 'saw . . . God' (verse 10) and 'beheld God' (verse 11).

We got pretty stuck trying to square this with John 1:18 ('No one has ever seen God') and with Exodus 33:20 ('man shall not see me and live'). Eventually we got rescued by a commentary (see Appendix on 'Commentaries, copying and catastrophe!') which suggested that they didn't *actually* see Yahweh at all. Let's try to explain . . .

A few years ago I (Andrew) was going for a walk with a friend in Green Park in London and stumbled accidentally upon the Trooping of the Colour – the British monarch's official birthday parade. I saw Her Majesty Queen Elizabeth II. I could just make out the wheels of her ivory-mounted phaeton carriage as it disappeared up The Mall towards Buckingham Palace.

Later that day I told my housemates I had 'seen' the Queen, when in actual fact I *didn't* see her, but only glimpsed her carriage. I wasn't lying; it's just a turn of phrase. Exodus 24 could be read in the same way. Verse 10 tells us that they saw God, but immediately it gets qualified – they saw the pavement under his feet. It seems they didn't (dare?) raise their eyes any higher than that. This shouldn't be taken as an anticlimax. The pavement itself is worthy of the **Tone and Feel tool**: it was 'as it were' a pavement of sapphire, 'like' a clear blue sky. It reminds us of another occasion in the Bible where someone 'saw Yahweh', and after a chapter of breathtaking imagery (drawn in part from Exodus 24), he confesses that what he has described was not the glory of Yahweh, nor the likeness of the glory of Yahweh, but the 'appearance of the likeness of the glory of Yahweh' (Ezekiel 1:28).

What does all of this mean for us?
Exodus 24 describes the ratification of the old covenant, sometimes called the 'Mosaic covenant' (though it has nothing to do with Roman tiled floors). It sets out the terms for life as the people of God, life within the bounds of his good law, life consecrated for his service, life in fellowship with him. And it's balanced on a knife edge.

At risk of ruining the suspense, the 'all-that-Yahweh-has-spoken-we-will-do' promise ends up sounding very hollow. The standard is too high. The human heart is too wicked. The beautiful relationship with God described in Exodus 24 seems beyond us.

How does all of this apply to us today? If we leave the **Bible Timeline tool** in the drawer and assume that nothing has changed as we move from Old to New Testament, then the lesson goes like this: 'You're God's holy people; he's holding out an amazing offer of relationship with him, provided you continue to walk in his ways, but you can't manage it because you are sinners, so the relationship is doomed.' If you think that's too pessimistic a view of things, just read on! The relationship looks doomed later in Exodus, and super-doomed by the time you get to 2 Kings.

But the relationship isn't doomed now. If we use the **Bible Timeline tool** with care, we discover that the coming of Jesus introduces at least three changes in the way we relate to God's law.

First, the law has fulfilled its role of bringing us to Christ. Listen to the apostle Paul:

> Is the law then contrary to the promises of God? Certainly not! For if a law had been given that could give life, then righteousness would indeed be by the law. But the Scripture imprisoned everything under sin, so that the promise by faith in Jesus Christ might be given to those who believe. Now before faith came, we were held captive under the law, imprisoned until the coming faith would be revealed. So then, the law was our guardian until Christ came, in order that we might be justified by faith. But now that faith has come, we are no longer under a guardian.
> (Galatians 3:21–25).

God never expected the Israelites to obey all of his commandments. He knew that they were sinful, that righteousness could never be achieved through their good works. The trouble is, *they* didn't realize it! They had every hope of reaching God by their own moral-ladder-climbing. And so it was that God set about teaching them a lesson. For the whole period of their history, stretching from the time of Moses to the birth of the baby in Bethlehem, he set the law over them as a 'guardian' (**Translations tool** suggested 'schoolmaster' or 'tutor') to convict them of their sin and show them their need of a saviour. Once we come to Jesus, the law has done its job.

Secondly, we have been delivered from the penalty of breaking the law. Listen to Paul again:

> For all who rely on works of the law are under a curse; for it is written, 'Cursed be everyone who does not abide by all things written in the Book of the Law, and do them.' Now it is evident that no one is justified before God by the law, for 'The righteous shall live by faith.' But the law is not of faith, rather 'The one who does them shall live by them.' Christ redeemed us from the curse of the law by becoming a curse for us – for it is written, 'Cursed is everyone who is hanged on a tree.'
> (Galatians 3:10–13)

Breaking God's law carried the death penalty. The Israelites broke the law, and so today do we, and so by nature all of us deserve God's judgment of death. But when Christ died on the cross (the 'tree'), he took the punishment ('the curse') that we deserved so that we might be spared. This puts us in a better position than those who gathered at Sinai, but the word 'better' needs to be nuanced: we ought not to think that they knew *nothing* of Christ's rescue, for they experienced at least a foreshadowing of it in the Passover. And we ought not to think that we can safely ignore warnings of judgment, for the consequences of wholesale rejection of God are just as terrifying now as they ever were (more on this when we look at how the New Testament applies Exodus 32).

In summary then, we no longer live 'under the law' as did the Israelites at the time of Moses: it no longer functions as our guardian, nor do we face its curse. This has convinced some that the law has no place at all in the life of a Christian, but that's hard to square with what we saw from Ephesians 6:2 and 1 Timothy 5:18 (see the previous discussion about the ongoing application of case law). There is a third aspect that we need to consider . . .

Thirdly, Christians have the law written on their hearts by God's Spirit. Hear Paul again:

> For when Gentiles, who do not have the law, by nature do what the law requires, they are a law to themselves, even though they do not have the law. They show that the work of the law is written on their hearts, while their conscience also bears witness, and their conflicting thoughts accuse or even excuse them.
> (Romans 2:14–15)

> For no one is a Jew who is merely one outwardly, nor is circumcision outward and physical. But a Jew is one inwardly, and circumcision is a matter of the heart, by the Spirit, not by the letter. His praise is not from man but from God.
> (Romans 2:28–29)

> Owe no one anything, except to love each other, for the one who loves another has fulfilled the law. For the commandments, 'You shall not commit adultery, You shall not murder, You shall not steal, You shall not covet', and any other commandment, are summed up in this word: 'You shall love your neighbour as yourself.' Love does no wrong to a neighbour; therefore love is the fulfilling of the law.
> (Romans 13:8–10)

These are tricky verses, but the **Quotation/Allusion tool** sniffs out the fulfilment of promises made in Deuteronomy and Jeremiah quicker than a French pig with a truffle. God had promised in Deuteronomy that 'Yahweh your God will circumcise your heart . . . so that you will love Yahweh your God . . . and you will keep all his commandments' (30:6–8). He had promised through Jeremiah that 'I will put my law within them, and I will write it on their hearts' (31:31–34). Now through the gospel, says Paul, this has become a reality. The holy life, set forth in God's law but once unattainable, becomes possible in the power of the Spirit.

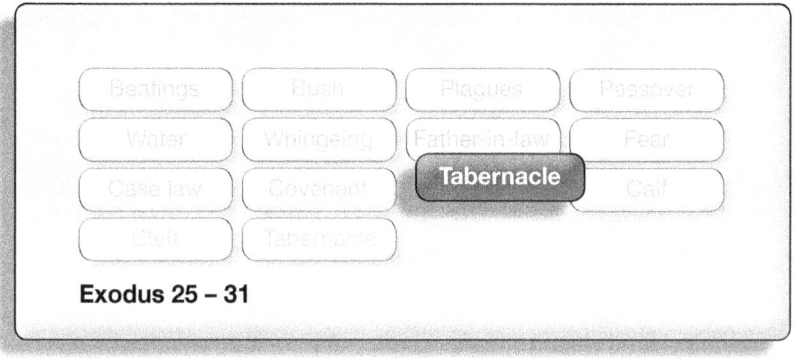

Exodus 25 – 31

How lovely is your dwelling place!
A guy in our congregation trades copper, aluminium and so forth on the Stock Exchange and ships it around the world. He tells us that, at the time of writing, he could get you the tonne of gold you'd need (working from the quantities given in Exodus 38:21–31) for $33m, the three and a half tonnes of silver for $1.75m and the two and half tonnes of bronze for $15,500. Sadly, his company doesn't deal in blue, purple and scarlet yarns, fine-twined linen, goats' hair, tanned rams' skins, goatskins, acacia wood, lamp oil, fragrant spices or onyx stones, so he couldn't quote us for those. 'And don't forget the cost of labour,' mutters a friend of ours bitterly, having just taken his car for a service. Granted, the bank balances of most Israelite families are in a rude state of health, thanks to the plundering of the Egyptians (12:35–36), but there's no denying the extravagance of the building project they are about to undertake.

Arm yourself with the **Tone and Feel tool** as you read over chapters 25 – 31. Look out for meticulous detail, fine craftsmanship and spectacular artistry. Look out for overlaying and engraving and weaving and embroidering. Consider the burnt offerings and sacrifices, the priests and their lavish clothes, the spices and their sweet fragrance. Do you catch a glimpse of the sheer *glory* of this place?

We tried the **Repetition tool** next (there's no magic formula for working out in advance which tools are going to be the most help with a given passage; it's often a case of just working your way through the toolkit to see what works best). For fun, we thought we'd put the **Repetition tool** on steroids and draw a diagram in which the size of a word is proportional to the number of times it is repeated in Exodus 25-31.

Figure 4

Pretty cool, eh? We shouldn't put toooo much trust in the **Repetition tool**, because the most important things aren't always said the most times, but it does give a flavour. The command to 'make' comes in first place with ninety-one hits – fairly unsurprising given that these are instructions about how to *make* the tabernacle. A couple of other repetitions give us more a sense of what kind of construction we're dealing with.

The first is the repetition of 'gold'. The ark is overlaid with gold, inside and out, and has cherubim hammered out of gold on its lid. There is a golden lampstand decorated with gold buds and gold branches. There are gold plates and dishes and pitchers and bowls. The priests wear a gold ephod and a gold breastpiece and are decorated with gold chains and gold bells. It seems there is a gold everything. You can't miss the splendour.

Another big hitter, just above the 'm' of 'make', is the word 'holy'. You can't read this section of Exodus and fail to notice that things are holy. There's a Holy Place and a Most Holy Place; there are holy garments and holy gifts and a holy crown and holy anointing oil. Almost everything in the tabernacle is holy or has to be 'consecrated' or 'sanctified' (that is, 'made holy').[1]

'Holy' is a word that comes up in a lot of Christian songs, but do we really know what it means? There are a couple of ways of using the **Vocabulary tool** to help. One is to delve into a reference book, such as the *New Bible Dictionary* (IVP), which helpfully explains that holiness is all about being separate or set apart. God himself is 'holy': he is separate both in his fundamental being (Creat-*or* as distinct from creat-*ed*) and in his moral purity ('God is light, and in him is no darkness at all', 1 John 1:5). Other things are 'holy' when they are set apart for divine use.

The other way of using the **Vocabulary tool** is simply to infer the meaning from the way the word is used. (Actually this is what the writers of the Bible dictionaries did!) We've seen already *in Exodus* that holiness is about God's separateness, his uniqueness among rivals: 'Who is like you, O Yahweh, among the gods? Who is like you, majestic in holiness?' (15:11). We've also seen that a place becomes holy, set apart, when Yahweh makes himself especially present there:

> God called to him out of the bush, 'Moses, Moses!' And he said, 'Here I am.' Then he said, 'Do not come near; take your sandals off your feet, for the place on which you are standing is holy ground.'
> (3:4–5)

By repeatedly describing the tabernacle and its furnishings as 'holy', the author is telling us that it is set apart for divine use. Perhaps he is even hinting that, like the burning bush, this is a place where Yahweh will make himself especially present with his people.

Quotation/Allusion tool

Like one of those activity books that your parents used to buy you for long car journeys, this is one of those 'match-things-in-the-left-column-with-the-jumbled-up-things-in-the-right-column' games. The pairs should be fairly obvious once you look up the verses.

Tabernacle	Genesis 1 – 3
The design of the lampstand (25:31–40).	The power of the Spirit of God to bring order from chaos (Genesis 1:2).
God 'says' things seven times (25:1; 30:11; 30:17; 30:22; 30:34; 31:1; 31:12) and the seventh one has something to do with Saturdays.	Cherubim guard the entrance to the garden (Genesis 3:24).

Tabernacle	Genesis 1 – 3
The embroidery on the curtain that screens off the Most Holy Place (26:31–33).	God 'finished', 'saw' and 'blessed' his work (Genesis 1:31 – 2:3).
Bezalel son of Uri son of Hur, and the reason behind his genius. Let's face it, had Bez been around when they were interviewing for the Sistine Chapel, Michelangelo would have ended up on the dole (31:1–11).	The garden has rich mineral resources, including gold and precious stones (Genesis 2:12).
The lavish materials used for the priests' clothing (28:15–30).	There is a tree of life in the middle of the garden (Genesis 2:9).
Moses' actions at the end of the construction project (39:32–43).	God makes the world in six days by speaking, and rests from all his work on the seventh day.

We think (and hopefully you now agree) that the writer of Exodus is going out of his way to identify the tabernacle with the garden of Eden.[2] But why?

- What was so good about God's creation of the world/ the garden of Eden?
- How do the creation/Eden allusions shape the way you view the tabernacle?

Another quick contribution from the **Vocabulary tool**, before you go fishing for herrings of a darker shade of pink: the 'ark' described in chapter 25 has nothing to do with the one used to rescue Moses in chapter 2 – it's altogether a different Hebrew word. In its own way, though, this ark is pretty amazing. It's home to the stone tablets with the Ten Commandments written on them, the visible symbol of Yahweh's covenant relationship with his people (25:16, 21). God promises to meet Moses there, and speak with him (25:22).

Next, an insight that the **Parallels tool** threw up back in chapter 15 (something we squirrelled away in our notebook in case it became important later on, now brought to mind courtesy of the **Context tool**):

> You will bring them in and plant them on your own mountain,
>   the place, O Yahweh, which you have made for your abode,
> the sanctuary, O Lord, which your hands have established.
> (15:17)

Whereas English poetry often rhymes, Hebrew poetry works by saying the same thing more than once in different words: 'Twinkle, twinkle little star/ / Shiny, shiny, tiny nebular'. In this example, the 'star' is the same as the 'nebular'; they are parallel expressions for the same reality. In the poem in Exodus 15, we have three expressions in parallel. The 'mountain' is the same as the place of God's 'abode', which is the same as his 'sanctuary'. Moses is equating the tabernacle with Sinai! The same reality of encounter with God, but without the geographical inflexibility (i.e. it's easier to take a tent with you on your travels than a mountain).

The construction of a gold-plated mobile palace didn't appear an obvious first priority for a nomadic people scraping out an existence in the desert. But let's summarize where we've got to: the tone and feel of the narrative speaks of the splendour of this tent. The repetition tells us of its holiness (amongst other things). Allusions to the opening chapters of Genesis conjure up images of a perfect world where God and humanity dwell in perfect relationship. The parallelism back in chapter 15 speaks of a portable Sinai.

The **Linking Word tool** takes us even further.

> Let them make me a sanctuary, *that* I may dwell in their midst.
> (Exodus 25:8)

Here is the reason for all of the gold! This is why the place is so holy, so Eden-like! The breathtaking truth is that Yahweh intends to dwell with his people. And all for a reason that by now should be very familiar:

> There I will meet with the people of Israel, and it shall be sanctified by my glory . . . I will dwell among the people of Israel and will be their God. *And they shall know that I am Yahweh* their God, who brought them out of the land of Egypt that I might dwell among them. *I am Yahweh* their God.
> (Exodus 29:43–46)

Yahweh is revealed not only in rescuing and judging, but also in dwelling among his people. It is fundamental to who he has revealed himself to be.

But that didn't mean that you could just waltz into God's presence whenever you felt like it. When the flag is flying at Buckingham Palace, you know that the Queen is dwelling in your midst, but that doesn't mean you're invited for tea! The footmen and the chambermaids are allowed in of course, but that's only because they have a particular job to do. So too with the priests here. They were responsible for bringing Jethro-like sacrifices of praise to God on behalf of the people.

But even the priests couldn't enter without extensive preparations. During their seven-day ordination service (chapter 29), the tabernacle resembled an abattoir more closely than a royal residence. The blood of a bull was poured out at the base of the altar, with some smeared on the horns of the altar with a finger (verse 12); the blood of a ram was sprinkled against the altar on all sides (verse 16); the blood of another ram was put 'on the tip of the right ear of Aaron and on the tips of the right ears of his sons, and on the thumbs of their right hands and on the great toes of their right feet' (verse 20). And to think that Andrew found his Church of England ordination an ordeal!

Why the rather gruesome procedure of dousing everything in ram's blood? The author explains that by these offerings 'atonement was made' (29:33). Similarly, the daily sacrifice of a bull was 'a sin offering for atonement' (29:36). No doubt Queen Elizabeth II has high standards of cleanliness, and a footman dutifully cleans your shoes before you are permitted to set foot on the Persian rugs (we're guessing here), but God's standards of cleanliness are higher still. Without atonement, no sinner may approach a holy God.

Blood and gore aside, the tabernacle was a great privilege. Living in the presence of God is what we were made for.

Andrew likes to fantasize sometimes about owning a time machine. OK, so he tried several times as a teenager to make one, using bits of dismantled household electronics. Let's humour him for a moment, and imagine you have one of these babies in your living room. You have the opportunity to try it just once. Where are you going to set the dial?

If you were really, really accurate, you might be able to arrive on the scene just in time for Passover night – careful though, or you'll end up making bricks for several years first. Turn the dial a few degrees further to the right and you'd get that once-in-a-lifetime opportunity to walk through the sea. A bit further still and you'd dine on posh chickens that fell out of the sky overnight or witness the Mount Sinai *Son et Lumière*. Impressive as they may be, we wouldn't go for any of these. We'd give the dial one more twist to be sure of seeing the completed tabernacle. What could be more glorious than looking out of your window each morning and seeing the dwelling place of Yahweh?

As the psalmist said later of the temple (the permanent structure that would replace the tabernacle when it didn't have to be portable any more because they had reached the Promised Land):

> How lovely is your dwelling place,
> > O Yahweh of hosts!
> My soul longs, yes, faints
> > for the courts of Yahweh;
> my heart and flesh sing for joy
> > to the living God.
> (Psalm 84:1–2)

Do we need cement mixers in Jerusalem?

Some people are so caught up with the beauty of the tabernacle/temple that, having no time machine, they plan to reconstruct it for the twenty-first century. Unfortunately, the chosen site in Jerusalem is currently home to the second holiest site in Islam, the Dome of the Rock mosque. Undeterred, they seek ultimately to evict the Muslims and re-establish the temple as the centre of God's blessing for the world. The movement is known as Christian Zionism and has many godly advocates. It also exerts great political influence, particularly in the United States. But we think it mistaken.

Tabernacle rebuilders haven't made sufficient use of the **Bible Timeline tool**. They've failed to consider whether anything changes as we move from Old to New Testament. Does someone who wants to meet with God today, who wants to offer a sacrifice to him, need to go on a pilgrimage to Jerusalem? No.

The original *Dig Deeper* explained that, to use the **Bible Timeline tool**, we have to ask three simple questions:

1. Where is this passage on the Bible timeline?
2. Where am I on the Bible timeline?
3. How do I read this in the light of things that have happened in between?

Has anything changed between (1) and (2)? Yes. At the coming of Jesus, everything changed for the temple. Everything changed for the way that human beings could approach God.

The Bible makes this point in so many places; we almost don't know where to start. For example:

- Jesus predicted the end of the temple (e.g. Mark 13) but not its rebuilding.
- Jesus invited the religious authorities to 'destroy this temple, and in three days I will raise it up' (John 2:19), but the narrator explains that 'he was speaking about the temple of his body' (John 2:21). The body of Jesus, and not the stone structure in Jerusalem, was the place of the final sacrifice for sin.
- In the amazing verse beloved of Christmas carol services, John says that 'the Word [Jesus] became flesh and *tabernacled* among us' (though you need the **Translations tool** to get this), i.e. the function once served by a tent is now served by a person.

- The apostle Paul uses temple language to refer not to buildings, but to a group of people in whom God dwells by his Spirit (Ephesians 2:22).

Thus the **Bible Timeline tool** urges us not to turn up in Jerusalem with hard hats, cement mixers and JCBs. Jesus' death once and for all upon the cross means that God now dwells by his Spirit *anywhere* that Christians gather in Jesus' name.

With us so far? Hope so, because this is one of the points in the book where we're going to hit the accelerator pretty hard.

So far we've noted that the Bible has one overarching story stretching from Genesis to Revelation. It pivots around the death and resurrection of Jesus, and the promises to Abraham, Isaac and Jacob superglue it all together. We've traced these promises through Exodus, but you can keep tracing all the way to the New Testament (e.g. Romans 4:16, 23–24; Galatians 3:8).

But there's another dimension to the Bible timeline. As we read the big story from beginning to end, we discover, like Russian dolls, miniature versions of the story hidden inside. Long before Jesus dies on a Roman cross and achieves for us 'redemption' (Colossians 1:14), we've seen the Israelites redeemed by the blood of a lamb. Long before Christ 'disarmed the rulers and authorities . . . triumphing over them' (Colossians 2:15), we've seen Pharaoh disarmed and triumphed over! The technical word for this is *typology*, which comes from the Greek word *typos* meaning 'pattern'. Typically (excuse the pun), the pattern comes in the Old Testament and the fulfilment in the New.

Sometimes the Bible describes the Old Testament preview as a 'shadow' of what is to come (Colossians 2:17; Hebrews 8:5; 10:1), which inspired Andrew to go on to Amazon and buy a book aimed at six-year-olds called *Whose Shadow Is This?* On one page you get a shadow ('Whose shadow is this, so lumpy and bumpy?'), and you turn the page and see the reality – a camel. You kick yourself when you see the porcupine ('that explains all those spikes!') or the giraffe ('no wonder it was so tall!'). While the shadow doesn't tell you everything, it's enough to recognize the reality when you see it. That's the point of typology.

Moses built a glorious tabernacle; God dwelt there among his people; the priests served there offering sacrifices. But we turn the page asking, 'Whose shadow is this?' and discover that the whole thing was a type, an anticipation of the ministry of our great High Priest, Jesus.

The book of Hebrews, though, takes the typology into (literally) a whole new dimension. The tabernacle wasn't just a copy of something to come *later*. It was a copy of something that wasn't man-made at all, not even part of this creation: a heavenly throne room.

> Now the point in what we are saying is this: we have such a high priest, one who is seated at the right hand of the throne of the Majesty in heaven, a minister in the holy places, in the true tent that the Lord set up, not man . . . [The earthly priests] serve a *copy and shadow* of the heavenly things. For when Moses was about to erect the tent, he was instructed by God, saying, 'See that you make everything according to the *pattern* that was shown you on the mountain.'
> (Hebrews 8:1–5; past masters of the **Quotation/Allusion tool** will pounce on the quotation from Exodus 25:40)

> Thus it was necessary for the *copies* of the heavenly things to be purified with [the sacrifices described in Exodus], but the heavenly things themselves with better sacrifices than these. For Christ has

entered, not into holy places made with hands, which are *copies* of the true things, but into heaven itself, now to appear in the presence of God on our behalf. Nor was it to offer himself repeatedly, as the high priest enters the holy places every year with blood not his own . . . But as it is, he has appeared once for all at the end of the ages to put away sin by the sacrifice of himself.
(Hebrews 9:23–26)

No wonder Moses was given such detailed instructions. No wonder there was so much gold. After all, this was God's heavenly palace they were copying. It was God's heavenly palace that Christ entered once and for all. And thanks to Jesus' sacrificial death, it is to God's heavenly palace that we now have access:

Therefore, brothers, since we have confidence to enter the holy places by the blood of Jesus, by the new and living way that he opened for us through the curtain, that is, through his flesh, and since we have a great priest over the house of God, let us draw near with a true heart in full assurance of faith, with our hearts sprinkled clean from an evil conscience and our bodies washed with pure water.
(Hebrews 10:19–22)

You can't really capture something as amazing as this in a diagram, but here's our best attempt:

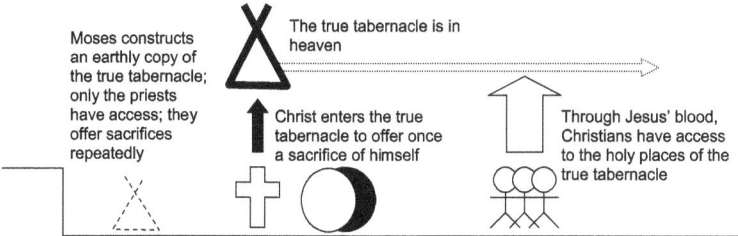

Figure 5

When we first thought about this, it was the mental equivalent of plugging twenty kettles into a two-amp socket and fusing the electrics of the whole street. Wow!

Picking ourselves off the floor, let's get out the **So What? tool** and ponder some of the implications of all this.

Implication 1. You don't need cement mixers in Jerusalem. Well you might, if you lived there and you were re-laying a patio or something, but you don't need one to build a temple. Perhaps the political landscape of the Middle East would look a little different if we all got that straight. God's throne room is in heaven, not in Jerusalem.

Implication 2. You don't need to go on a pilgrimage to the Holy Land to get closer to God. By all means go there for a fantastic holiday and get a feel for the biblical sites, as Andrew did last Easter with Oak Hall Expeditions (deliberate plug here: their Israel trip really is excellent). By all means go to Glastonbury to enjoy the rock concert or to Lourdes to practise your French. But don't go to any of these places expecting God to be closer to you. God's throne room is in heaven, not in Israel, Somerset or France.

Implication 3. You don't need a gold rope to mark off the 'special bit' of church, where only the vicar is allowed to go. For that matter, you don't need an 'altar' in church, and you don't need the vicar to wear priestly garments, and unless you particularly like the smell (we don't), you don't need to burn incense. All of these practices are lifted from Exodus 25 – 31 and applied directly to the church building in your village, or the cathedral in our city – Westminster Abbey even has a sign on the door telling you that you're entering the 'house of God'. There is zero biblical precedent for this. And why on earth would you go back to shadows when you possess the reality?

Both Andrew and his mum were converted in Cambridge, partly through the ministry of the Round Church. The building is very old (it was constructed by the Knights Templar during the Crusades) and very solid (supported by vast stone pillars) and very dark. In fact, a totally unviable place for a congregation to meet, which is why they're now down the road in the refurbished buildings of St Andrew the Great. The story goes that decades ago, in response to a spate of thefts, the police decided to hide a constable up in the rafters, in the gloomy centre of the church. It was a great vantage point; he could see everything, but no-one on the ground could see him. Sure enough, the thief entered, picked the lock on the collection box, and made off down the road. There he was apprehended by two more police officers. Needing an eyewitness verification of the crime, they frogmarched the culprit back to the church and looked up to heaven. 'Is this the fella?' they asked. Assisted by the ancient acoustic, the voice that came back from the shadows boomed like thunder, 'Yes, that's him.' You can imagine the look of terror on the face of the man who thought he'd met his Maker.

It's a fun story, and probably apocryphal. But it works on the assumption that, if God could be found anywhere in Cambridge, he'd be sure to choose for his dwelling somewhere with musty smells and stained glass. The more ancient the better. But the notion that God lives at the Round Church is as unfounded as the idea that Santa lives in Lapland. (Sorry, children, but this is a joint conspiracy between the Royal Mail and the Lapland Tourist Board.) God's throne room is in heaven, not in Cambridge.

Implication 4. You don't need a worship leader to usher you into God's presence with uplifting worship and Spirit-filled chords at Soul Survivor or New Word Alive. If God had intended us to be brought near to him through music, then Jesus could have spared himself the agony of Calvary and learned the guitar. Please forgive us for putting that so starkly. We're not wishing to denigrate music, which is a precious gift to the church. We're not wishing to deny the joy of singing God's praises or the exhilaration of doing so in the company of great crowds. But when what *we do* in our Christian meeting competes with what *Jesus has done*, we are in danger. God's throne room is in heaven, and Jesus has won us access once and for all.

We've given some negative implications, but really these are just the flipside of one enormous positive. We have access to the heavenly throne room of God through Christ our High Priest. It is because he is sufficient that we have no need of anything else.

Here's a Muslim. Wants to know Allah better. Has to trek to the Kiblah in Mecca. Too old to travel. Poor him. Here's a Christian. Wants to know God better. Has to trek to St Paul's Cathedral in London. Too old to travel. Poor her. No, wait a minute. She doesn't have to go anywhere! Here she is in her armchair, a prayer away from the throne room of heaven.

In summary, Moses' tabernacle is the shadow that points forward to

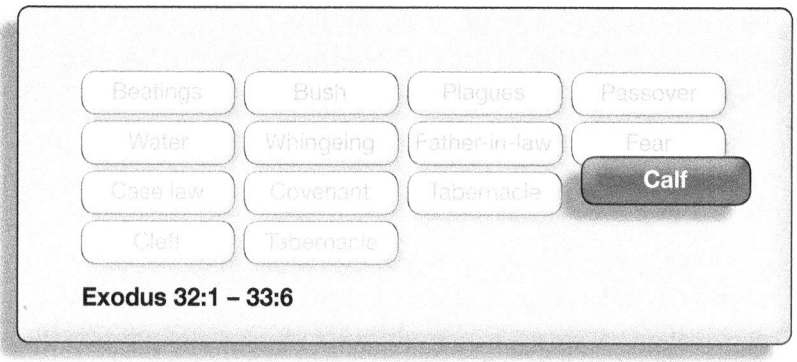

Exodus 32:1 – 33:6

In case you're wondering, the nice people at IVP didn't make a mistake when typesetting the last chapter. The decision to end abruptly in mid-sentence was deliberate. We've heard the design specifications, but before work can start, before Moses even gets down the mountain with the architectural drawings, there is a terrible interruption.

The plot of the chapter is pretty obvious. The Israelites mess up very badly. Yahweh is angry. Moses prays. But people still die. We don't need the toolkit to get these basics, but we can use it to deepen our understanding.

The Israelites mess up very badly
Andrew was in York for his PhD. It's a beautiful historic city with its ancient Minster and city walls dating back to Roman times. Confusingly, the roads are called 'gates' and the gates (in the city walls) are called 'bars'. His favourite road was Whip-ma-whop-ma-gate (just because of the ridiculous name), and

his favourite gate was Monk Bar (because it was a short walk from the terraced house painted with an old advert for 'Nightly Bile Beans: Keep you healthy, bright-eyed and slim'). But enough of the nostalgia. The point of Andrew indulging his York memories is to tell you about the horrors of what 1960s architecture did to King's Manor, an exquisite Elizabethan building next to the Museum Gardens. If you haven't been there, think Oxbridge quad from the movies. Imagine the travesty of slicing off the top storey and replacing it with a concrete structure resembling a multi-storey car park. Yes, somebody did this. The supreme irony? This building is now home to a university department where you can study for an MA in Conservation of Historic Buildings. The one redeeming feature of the modern additions is a rather nice cast statue of a calf in the middle of the courtyard.

But back in Exodus, it was the calf that was the unsightly eyesore. The gold intended for the tabernacle was put to a very different use. Worse than what concrete can do to a sixteenth-century courtyard is what human sin can do to a beautiful relationship with God.

The Israelites' behaviour provokes Moses to smash the stone tablets on which God had written the Ten Commandments (32:15–19). That's enough of a hint for us to turn to the **Context tool** to consider which of those Commandments has been broken. There are two obvious candidates:

1. 'You shall have no other gods before me' (20:3).

The first option is that the Israelites have turned aside from Yahweh to worship a calf-god instead. But this seems almost inconceivable. It's only a matter of months since they walked through the Red Sea. Is it really possible that they should have forgotten which god was responsible for their rescue?

> II. 'You shall not make for yourself a carved image, or any likeness of anything . . . You shall not bow down to them or serve them' (20:4–5).

The second option is that they *think* that they are worshipping Yahweh. They haven't, consciously at least, broken the first commandment at all. The issue is the second commandment: they've decided to represent God as an image of their choosing. Perhaps they imagine he would be flattered that they chose a calf – such a strong and noble animal. Perhaps they imagine he would be flattered that they made it from gold.

In which direction does the text point? At first sight, the reference to 'gods' (plural) in verses 1, 4, 8, 23 seems to favour the first option. The Israelites have done a kind of reverse-Jethro, and turned aside from Yahweh to embrace polytheism. Odd though, if the emphasis is on many gods, why do they make only one calf? Why not a golden herd?

The **Translations tool** makes a useful contribution here. Remember that it's always a good idea to be checking another translation, just in case. This is what we found in the New American Standard Bible: 'This is your *god*, O Israel, who brought you up from the land of Egypt' (32:4, 8, NASB).

Right. So it seems that singular/plural thing isn't decisive either way. The Israelites could be talking about Yahweh after all. Indeed, it's hard to think of who else they could be thinking of when they speak of the calf bringing them out of Egypt – surely Yahweh's signature move. And as they get the altar and burnt offerings ready, Aaron's announcement clinches it:

> Tomorrow shall be a feast to Yahweh.
> (32:5)

In conclusion, the whole golden-calf episode is intended as worship of Yahweh. Yahweh reshaped and re-conceptualized as a calf, but Yahweh nonetheless.

The **Context tool** helps us to understand the Yahweh-as-calf mindset. At the top of the mountain, Yahweh told them what he was like, and therefore how to live in relationship with him (20:1–17). At the bottom of the mountain, the people make a few modifications. First they redefine Yahweh as a calf, and then they get to choose what kinds of ethics calf-Yahweh would demand of them. It turns out (surprise, surprise) that calf-Yahweh's moral standards are a little looser:

> The people sat down to eat and drink and rose up to play.
> (32:6)

A euphemism if ever there was one! It's a mad orgy, basically. The party gets so out of control that they become a laughing stock to their enemies (32:25). But the heart of the issue is what we might call an 'anti-Sinai', a rejection of all God had revealed about himself.

To consider just how much this insults God, we return to the silly analogy that we began a few chapters back. Andrew is telling Richard how he likes Beethoven and vintage port, but doesn't like Formula One or death metal. And Richard responds:

> 'Did you watch the Bahrain Grand Prix at the weekend?'
> 'No, Richard. I'm not keen on Formula One, like I said.'
> 'Yeah, you are. You love it. You're a huge Ferrari fan.'

> *Andrew doesn't get the joke, but gives a little laugh and tries to change the subject.* 'So anyway, I hear that Charlie has started crawling?'
> 'Yeah, it's cool. That Lewis Hamilton overtaking manoeuvre was amazing, wasn't it? He almost sent Button into the tyres.'
> 'Richard, I'm not into Formula One. I didn't watch it.'
> 'Yes you did.'
> 'Mate, are you calling me a liar?'
> 'I'm just saying you love Formula One.'

It's not a recipe for a happy friendship. But it's a lot worse with the God version.

> 'So Jesus, there are lots of ways to God, aren't there? You're just one of them.'
> 'I am the way, and the truth, and the life. No one comes to the Father except through me.'
> 'You think Hinduism and Islam are just as valid though, don't you, Jesus? Anyway, must get going, can't wait to see my girlfriend in that lingerie I bought her.
> 'Everyone who looks at a woman with lustful intent has already committed adultery with her in his heart.'
> 'Oh come off it, Jesus, you don't really believe that. As long as it makes me happy, you're happy, right?'

The attraction of a design-your-own God is design-your-own ethics. At Sinai, God gives his rules for how to live. At anti-Sinai not all of the rules apply. Just the ones you like. Our culture agrees that murder is still wrong but thinks that sexual immorality is OK, and so we come up with a calf-Yahweh who gives us only nine commandments, with number seven conveniently missing. That seems to be what happened with the Israelites. In a sanitized description designed to spare our blushes, the author simply says they 'rose up to play' (verse 6). You don't need us to spell out the graphic details.

All of this makes Yahweh angry.

Yahweh is angry

In perhaps the most sobering event in the whole of the book of Exodus, Moses assembles a Levite execution squad and issues a terrifying order:

> And he said to them, 'Thus says Yahweh God of Israel, "Put your sword on your side each of you, and go to and fro from gate to gate throughout the camp, and each of you kill his brother and his companion and his neighbour."'
>
> (32:27)

These are emergency measures for a desperate situation. It might seem extreme to us, but the text is clear that the Levites' actions receive the approval of Yahweh (verse 29). In fact, without their intervention to stop the idolatrous festival dead in its tracks, the final death toll might have been higher still: that's the implication of the closely related episode in Numbers 25:1–9. (Have a look.)

Just a note of warning here if you are squeamish about the idea of God's judgment, if your fingers are curling into a fist to shake at him in defiance: it was gentle Jesus, meek and mild, who spoke of hell as a place of torment and fire (Luke 16:23–24) and told of many on the broad road to destruction (Matthew 7:13). We are assured repeatedly in the Bible that his judgment is proportionate, and if we fail to see this, then we've not begun to understand the heinousness of our crimes. If you've made for yourself a god who doesn't get angry enough to react like he does in Exodus 32, then you're looking at a calf-Yahweh of your own imagination.

While the Levite execution squad is the most graphic manifestation of God's anger, it is not the only one.

Context tool

How is the seriousness of the following judgments revealed by their context?

- God's description of the Israelites, when talking to Moses, as '*your* people, whom *you* brought up out of Egypt' (32:7) in the wider context of 12:51; 16:6; 20:2.

- Moses' clumsy accident with some stonework (32:19) in the immediate context of 32:15–16.

- The plague sent on the Israelites (32:35) in the wider context of . . . no, this is too obvious for us to give you verse numbers!

- God's announcement that he will send an angel instead of accompanying the people personally (33:2–3), in the immediate context of how the Israelites receive this news (33:4–6) and in the wider context of 25:8; 29:45–46.

There is one more consequence that is easily missed. Idolatry doesn't just anger God. It also corrupts the idolater. We were about to use the **Vocabulary tool** to get to the bottom of the description of the Israelites as 'stiff-necked' when we came across Greg Beale's recent tome, *We Become What We Worship* (Apollos):

> When the first generation of Israel worshipped the golden calf, Moses describes them in a manner that sounds like they are being portrayed as wild calves or untrained cows: they became (1) stiff necked (Exodus 32:9; 33:3, 5; 34:9) and would not obey, but (2) they 'were let loose' because 'Aaron had let them go loose' (Exodus 32:25), (3) so that 'they had quickly turned aside from the way,' (Exodus 32:8) and they needed to be (4) 'gathered together' again 'in the gate' (Exodus 32:26), (5) so that Moses could 'lead the people where' God had told them to go (Exodus 32:34).[1]

The Israelites are 'stiff-necked' because they have come to resemble the calf-idol they made. God made us in his image, and to reflect his character is to be truly human. But to distort his character soon distorts ours. We find ourselves dehumanized.

The consequences of making God in your image are devastating. And in 1 Corinthians Paul wants to make sure we learn the lesson of Exodus 32 (**Quotation/Allusion tool** meets **So What? tool**):

> Now these things took place as examples for us, that we might not desire evil as they did. Do not be idolaters as some of them were; as it is written, 'The people sat down to eat and drink and rose up to play.'
> (1 Corinthians 10:6–7, quoting Exodus 32:6)

Idolatry of the calf-Yahweh kind is dangerous because it's so subtle. Few of us are tempted simply to switch gods ('I used to worship Jesus, but now I worship Zeus'). But we are tempted to airbrush those Bible truths we find inconvenient, to make a few adjustments, to accommodate God to our culture and our lifestyle. This way, we can still retain the name Christian, keep going to church, keep singing our favourite worship songs. We may even convince ourselves that God doesn't mind.

Don't do it, says Paul. God does mind. Look at what happened to Israel.

Moses prays
When God threatens to consume the people in his wrath and to make a new start with Moses (verse 10), Moses pleads with him to reconsider:

> O Yahweh, why does your wrath burn hot against your people, whom you have brought out of the land of Egypt with great power and with a mighty hand? Why should the Egyptians say, 'With evil intent did he bring them out, to kill them in the mountains and to consume them from the face of the earth'? Turn from your burning anger and relent from this disaster against your people. Remember Abraham, Isaac, and Israel, your servants, to whom you swore by your own self, and said to them, 'I will multiply your offspring as the stars of heaven, and all this land that I have promised I will give to your offspring, and they shall inherit it forever.'
> (32:11–13)

Unfortunately this passage has become a happy hunting ground for a bunch of rogue teachers who call themselves 'Open Theists'. They think that God is so concerned not to tread on the toes of human freedom that he's willing to surrender his control of the world and even his knowledge of the future. Consequently, God is often caught out by human actions and has to change his plans. 'Look,' they say, 'God was planning to punish Israel, but he's forced to do a U-turn when he hears Moses' persuasive counterarguments. He never foresaw that.'

Time for the **Author's Purpose tool**. Is this really consistent with the overall picture the author has been painting of the relationship between Yahweh and Moses? Moses in the driving seat? Moses pulling the strings? Erm, no. Read Exodus 3 – 4 again if you need a refresher. It was Yahweh's idea to rescue his people, and he is committed to keeping his promises. Does the author really intend to undermine all of that?

Fact is, Exodus isn't the best target for someone wanting to undermine the truth of God's absolute control over his world. The book resonates with it. As a little miscellaneous example, check out 34:22–24 where Yahweh invites all the men of Israel to gather for the major feasts. You only have to ponder it for a moment to realize this is suicide in terms of national security. What? *All* the men? Including those who defend the border? But Yahweh silences these concerns with an extraordinary promise: 'No one shall covet your land, when you go up to appear before Yahweh three times in the year.' God is so much in control that he can overrule even the *desires* of neighbouring hostile nations.

We can see evidence that God is in control of the situation here, even as Moses persuades him to relent. First, Moses only gets down to prayer because God tells him of what is about to happen to the Israelites, and asks Moses to 'let me alone' (verse 10). What? Since when did God need to be 'let alone' before he could do something? It seems to us that God is giving Moses a *whopping hint* that a few prayers wouldn't go amiss. To paraphrase:

> 'I'm going to destroy everyone Moses, if that's OK with you, so if you'd be so kind as to just step aside and let me get on with it. Unless you've anything to say on the matter? Have you? Moses? MOSES?'

Secondly, the prayer itself is full of themes that God has drilled into Moses, almost as if rehearsing him for this very moment: Moses appeals to Yahweh on the basis of his *covenant promises* (verse 13). Ironically for those who argue from these verses that God changes his mind, Moses is pleading that God won't do that! Don't change your mind, Yahweh. Please stick with your plans.

And so in verse 14, Yahweh relents from his threat but sticks with his promise. The people are spared.

But people still die

Some think that God has given them a safety net so wide that they are free to skip along the tightrope of sin without a care in the world: 'It doesn't matter if I sin, because God will always forgive me.' It would be possible to read Exodus 32 in that kind of way. The Israelites mess up very badly; God is angry; Moses prays, and everything is OK.

But everything is not OK. The author is at pains to show us that Moses' prayer, while averting disaster for the nation as a whole, does not let everyone off scot-free.

When we first used the **Structure tool** in this chapter, we wanted everything to be neat and tidy. We expected a simple 'before' and 'after', where everything bad came in the first half (before Moses' prayer) and everything good came after it. But it just didn't work like that. Did you notice, for example, that the Levite execution squad is despatched *after* Moses prays? And then he prays again (presumably conscious that God's anger had not been entirely quenched), and then there is a plague.

In other words, the structure we expected was:

Execution squad
Plague
Prayer
Everything is OK

But the structure that we actually find is:

Prayer
Execution squad
Prayer
Plague

We were so tempted to rearrange the passage! Instead, we got out the **Author's Purpose tool** and began wrestling with why on earth he would have chosen to write it like this. Originally we thought that this was a point of contrast between Moses and Jesus. Moses enjoys *some* success as a mediator – in response to his prayers, God relents from wiping out Israel altogether (verse 14) – but his powers are limited. He cannot save *completely*. In particular, when he offers to give his own life as a ransom for many, he overstretches himself:

> So Moses returned to Yahweh and said, 'Alas, this people has sinned a great sin. They have made for themselves gods of gold. But now, if you will forgive their sin – but if not, please blot me out of your book that you have written.' But Yahweh said to Moses, 'Whoever has sinned against me, I will blot out of my book.'
> (32:31–33)

Where Moses fails, Jesus succeeds. No plagues or execution squads come after those whom Jesus has prayed for. He successfully offers his life as a substitute for God's people, and as a result he is able to free us 'from everything from which you could not be freed by the law of Moses' (Acts 13:39). It makes a good little sermon, and Andrew has preached it that way.

But then we changed our minds. It would be odd for the author to be making a point about the inadequacy of Moses as a swap for sinful people, when in chapter 12 God was prepared to accept the blotting out of a mere animal – a lamb – as an adequate sacrifice. Odd too because in the next chapter (as we shall see) the author will emphasize the success of Moses' mediation, and we will find ourselves drawing positive comparisons, rather than a contrast, with the work of Jesus.

There is another option. The point of the execution squad and the plague coming after Moses' prayer is not to denigrate the work of Moses at all. Rather, it's a warning that those who fall away completely put themselves beyond God's forgiveness. When we looked again at 1 Corinthians 10 (the passage we considered above using the **Quotation/Allusion tool**), we realized that this is exactly right. Paul writes to those who already call themselves Christians, and warns them that they cannot walk safely down the tightrope of sin. If you fall away from Jesus, then the blood of Jesus won't help you any more than the blood of Moses could help the Israelites.

When it comes to walking tightropes, the author's purpose is clear. Don't do it.

> **BRAINBOX ASIDE: More calves**
>
> Read 1 Kings 12:28–29. What is Jeroboam up to? Has he read Exodus 32? It would seem too much of a coincidence if not, but if he has read it . . . ? What is going on in his head?
>
> Happy digging!

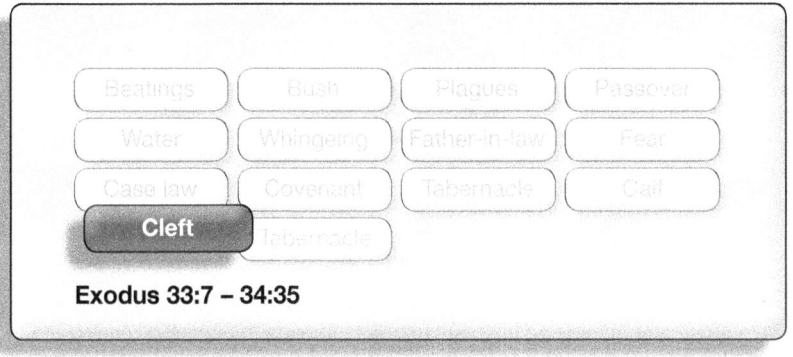

Exodus 33:7 – 34:35

Will it ever be the same again?
If you've ever done something to jeopardize a close friendship, you'll know that it's one of the worst feelings in the world. It's a stomach-churning, wake-in-the-middle-of-the-night feeling. It's an 'if-only, if-only' feeling. All you want is for things to be the same, but you don't know if they *can* be the same.

That's exactly how I (Richard) felt the time I hit my next-door neighbour in the face with a golf club. It was an accident, of course. We were on the green, a couple of yards from the hole, and the ball just needed a nudge. So you can understand why my friend, standing just behind me, wasn't prepared for my full back swing. He was furious, burst into tears, and ran home to his mum. (We were about eight years old.) I was left standing there, contemplating the end of our friendship. I guess that's pretty much how the Israelites felt at the beginning of Exodus 33.

Granted, things aren't quite as bad as they were in the last chapter, when Yahweh threatened to kill them. But that doesn't mean he's enthusiastic about being friends. Every Israelite asks himself, 'Can it ever be the same again?'

Chapter 33 verses 7–11 offer the first glimmer of hope: Moses sets up a tent and calls it a 'tent of meeting'. Armed with the **Context tool**, the mention of camping equipment gets us thinking back to the tabernacle, and we're excited. This *isn't* the tabernacle, it's important to understand – no gold, no embroidery, no tanned rams' skins – but it's a tent nonetheless. After the golden calf we were expecting the whole tabernacle project to be called off, but already God is continuing with something (a bit) like it.

The tent of meeting, though, is 'outside the camp' (verse 7), whereas the plan for the tabernacle was for God to be 'in their midst' (25:8). Things aren't quite the same. While *Moses* is friends with God (verse 11) – seemingly he pops in for a chat with Yahweh whenever it takes his fancy – we still don't know where the people stand. There's an air of wistfulness as they look on from a distance:

> Whenever Moses went out to the tent, all the people would rise up, and each would stand at his tent door, and watch Moses until he had gone into the tent.
> (verse 8)

> And when all the people saw the pillar of cloud standing at the entrance of the tent, all the people would rise up and worship, each at his tent door.
> (verse 10)

It's a kind of halfway-house tabernacle, and a halfway-house relationship.

Moses intercedes

Moses is the only one in Yahweh's good books, and he and Yahweh seem to be spending a lot of time together. Wouldn't you love to be a fly on the wall (or on the canvas)? What was Moses up to in the tent of meeting? In verses 12–17 we're given the chance to eavesdrop:

> 'Please let the people go to the land you promised'. 'Please come with us to the land.' 'Yahweh, please don't just be *my* God, but continue to be *our* God' (our paraphrase).

Repetition tool

Read Exodus 33:12–17. Use the **Repetition tool** to identify the basis on which Moses appeals to Yahweh and on which Yahweh grants his request (the phrase comes five times).

As a result of Moses' intercession, the people end up sharing in the favour he enjoys with Yahweh. To start with, only he had that special relationship. But it became theirs too because they came to share in what was his.

Experienced **Who am I? tool** users will be quick to identify themselves not with the one doing the praying but with the ones being prayed for. We are not Moses in this story. But there is someone else in the Bible who intercedes for his people on the basis of the favour he himself enjoys with God. The setting is an upper room in Jerusalem the night before the crucifixion. Once again we are allowed to eavesdrop:

> Father . . . The glory *that you have given me* I have given to them.
> (John 17:21–22)

> O righteous Father . . . I made known to them your name . . .
> that the love *with which you have loved me* may be in them.
> (John 17:25–26)

As a result of Jesus' intercession, we end up sharing in the favour he enjoys with his Father. To start with, only he had that special relationship. But it becomes ours too because we come to share in what was his.

We've got some more stuff to say, but when you've just thought about something as awesome as our sharing in Jesus' glory, it doesn't seem quite right just to carry on typing. We're going to go for a walk and pray about this. We suggest you do the same.

Yes, but is it really, really OK?

A little bit of us is still thinking, *surely* the Israelites can't have been forgiven that easily after all they did? It's too good to be true. Yahweh delivered them from Egypt and smashed their enemies, and the Israelites gave all the credit to a statue, and Yahweh forgave them just like that – how can it possibly be? Even Moses can't get his head around it.

When Moses says, 'Please show me your glory' (33:18), he's asking for reassurance. He's looking for some kind of knock-out experience to convince him that Yahweh means what he says and everything really is OK. And he gets one. Though at first it looks like a bit of an anticlimax.

Andrew's been to the Royal Opera House in London a couple of times to hear his friend Katie Van Kooten, an opera singer, performing. Unfortunately, they didn't have C of E clergy in mind when setting the ticket prices, so this meant going for the seats that they advertise as 'Restricted View'. No kidding. If you crane your neck, the most you can hope for is a glimpse of the third trombone – and even then only when he extends the slide to reach a low note. Katie sounded good though.

Moses' view of God's glory passing by makes Andrew's view at Covent Garden look panoramic by comparison. The cleft in the rock (verse 22) wasn't the most promising vantage point at the best of times, but when Yahweh decided to cover the entrance with his hand, not so much as a photon of glory-light would have made it to Moses' retina (admittedly for important health and safety reasons, verse 20). In other words, Moses sits in pitch darkness throughout the whole thing. He only gets to see God's 'back' after it's all over, which is equivalent to getting a good view of the safety curtain after it's fallen for the last time.

Moses sees nothing. But he hears something absolutely breathtaking. If you could condense God's glory into fifty-seven words (only thirty-two in Hebrew!), they would sound like this:

> Yahweh, Yahweh, a God merciful and gracious, slow to anger, and abounding in steadfast love and faithfulness, keeping steadfast love for thousands, forgiving iniquity and transgression and sin, but who will by no means clear the guilty, visiting the iniquity of the fathers on the children and the children's children, to the third and the fourth generation.
> (Exodus 34:6–7)

The most glorious thing Yahweh can show Moses is his name, and this gives Moses all the reassurance he needs. Of course the Israelites have been forgiven. Of course the relationship has been restored. Of course everything is OK. This is *Yahweh* we're dealing with.

Anyone else having a **Context tool**-inspired sense of déjà vu? This is another burning-bush moment, a 'please-convince-me-that-you-really-mean-this' moment. And just like at the burning bush, God's answer is to proclaim his name. In fact, God's name is the answer to everything in Exodus. It's the theme tune, and by now we should all be singing along.

Exodus 34:6–7 represents perhaps the fullest explanation of God's name in the whole of the Old Testament. The Israelites come back to it over and over again, so much so that your **Quotation/Allusion tool** gets worn out. It becomes a favourite chorus in some of their praise songs, like Psalm 103 or Psalm 145:

> Yahweh is merciful and gracious,
>   slow to anger and abounding in steadfast love.
> (Psalm 103:8)

> Yahweh is gracious and merciful,
>   slow to anger and abounding in steadfast love.
> (Psalm 145:8)

They use it to comfort themselves when they are scared, like in Psalm 86 (written at the time when David was hiding from those who sought to kill him):

> But you, O Yahweh are a God merciful and gracious,
>   slow to anger and abounding in steadfast love and faithfulness.
> (Psalm 86:15)

The prophet Joel uses it to call people back to God, when they have wandered off in sin:

> Return to Yahweh, your God,
>   for he is gracious and merciful,
> slow to anger, and abounding in steadfast love.
> (Joel 2:13)

The prophets Jonah and Nahum both use it in connection with God's judgment on the evil city of Nineveh. Jonah uses it to remind himself that God is patient with sinners (which he finds hard to stomach):

> [God's sparing of Nineveh] displeased Jonah exceedingly, and he was angry . . . 'I knew that you are a gracious God and merciful, slow to anger and abounding in steadfast love, and relenting from disaster.'
> (Jonah 4:1–2).

Nahum uses it to warn that God's patience eventually runs out:

> Yahweh is slow to anger and great in power,
>   and Yahweh will by no means clear the guilty.
> (Nahum 1:3)

Moses himself comes back to it, when for a second time he finds himself interceding for a rebellious people:

> Yahweh is slow to anger and abounding in steadfast love, forgiving iniquity and transgression, but he will by no means clear the guilty, visiting the iniquity of the fathers on the children, to the third and the fourth generation.
> (Numbers 14:18)

If you want a memory verse, this is it. If you want a bumper sticker, this would be even better than the one that says, 'If you can read this, I've lost my caravan' (Andrew's personal favourite). Get it made into a fridge magnet. Set it as your screensaver. Make it your facebook status update. Tweet it. Do anything you can to imprint these words in your memory, and pray for us that we'd do the same.

Proof that it's OK

'Can it ever be the same?' asked the Israelites. Yes, says the author, and in various ways he shows us that things are now back on track. What's been restored is only apparent against the backdrop of what they had originally and what they lost. We need the **Context tool here**.

Context: What they had	Context: What they lost because of the calf	Chapter 34
Stone tablets representing the covenant that God made with them (31:18).	The stone tablets are smashed (32:19).	New stone tablets (34:1, 28; accomplished **Structure tool** users will notice that these references bracket the whole section).
Rites and festivals to commemorate how Yahweh brought them out of Egypt: specifically the Passover, Feast of Unleavened Bread and Consecration of the Firstborn (12:1 – 13:16).	The people attribute the rescue from Egypt to the calf (32:4). Yahweh responds by attributing the rescue to Moses, refusing to identify himself as their Saviour (32:7).	Renewed mention of rites and festivals that commemorate how Yahweh brought them out of Egypt: specifically the Feast of Unleavened Bread (34:18), Consecration of the Firstborn (34:19–20) and Passover (34:25).

Context: What they had	Context: What they lost because of the calf	Chapter 34
When Moses descends Sinai, having met God to receive the tablets of the law, the people respond rightly in fear (20:18–21).	When Moses descends the mountain, the people are engaged in idolatrous revelry (32:18–19).	When Moses descends Sinai having met God to receive tablets of the law, the people respond rightly in fear (34:30).
Plans for a tabernacle whereby God would dwell in the midst of the people (25:8–9).	Moses meets God in a tent outside of the camp; the people stand at a distance (33:7–11).	Read on for more details of how the original tabernacle is back on track

It seems everything is back to normal. There's almost no trace of what had gone wrong, except for the rather pointed rewording of the second commandment: 'You shall not make for yourselves any gods of cast metal' (34:17).

On the whole though, all that was broken has been wonderfully mended. How come? Because of Yahweh. Because he is gracious and merciful. Because he abounds in steadfast love. Because he forgives iniquity and transgression and sin.

Veiled and unveiled faces

After forty days and forty nights with Yahweh on the mountain, Moses descends with a face resembling a lighthouse (34:29–30), an effect that Andrew can now achieve sometimes on a sunny day, thanks to advanced baldness (thanks for that, Richard). When speaking to the people, Moses veils his face to shield them from the glory-radiance. When speaking to Yahweh, he unveils his face (verses 33–35).

The **Context tool** is always close at hand, and so reading about veiled faces made us think immediately of the cleft, and how Moses can't look at God's face directly (33:20). There seems to be a double-distancing of God's glory from the people:

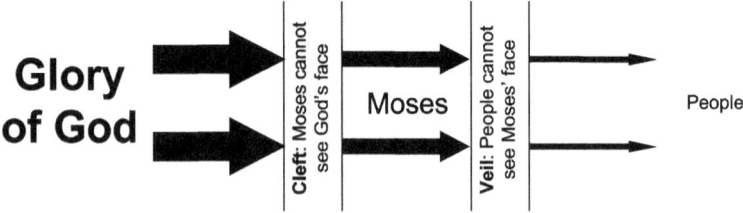

Figure 6

We shouldn't think of this too negatively. The fact is, although Moses isn't allowed to see God's face, he still speaks to him 'face to face, as a man speaks to his friend' (33:11) and emerges with his own face shining. Although the Israelites can't manage to look at Moses for too long, they seem to catch glimpses of his radiance before he veils it (34:35). Some glory gets through from the left of the diagram, just not all of it.[1]

The strange thing is, this still sounds like the halfway-house relationship with which we began in 33:7–11. Moses goes into the tent of meeting to talk with God; the people stand at a distance. Certainly some things have changed – we've got a new revelation of God's character, new stone tablets, a glory-glowing-face – but we still need Moses as a go-between. The relationship with Yahweh is restored but never unmediated.

We turn finally to the **Quotation/Allusion tool** to bring things to an end with a bang. In 2 Corinthians 3, Paul makes reference to our verses from Exodus:

> Since we have such a hope, we are very bold, not like Moses, who would put a veil over his face so that the Israelites might not gaze at the outcome of what was being brought to an end. But their minds were hardened. For to this day, when they read the old covenant, that same veil remains unlifted, because only through Christ is it taken away. Yes, to this day whenever Moses is read a veil lies over their hearts. But when one turns to the Lord, the veil is removed. Now the Lord is the Spirit, and where the Spirit of the Lord is, there is freedom. And we all, with unveiled face, beholding the glory of the Lord, are being transformed into the same image from one degree of glory to another. For this comes from the Lord who is the Spirit. (2 Corinthians 3:12–18)

Paul draws a contrast here between 'we' and Moses. We assumed that 'we' meant Christians in general, but when we checked using the **Context tool**, we found it was more specifically a reference to Paul and Timothy (the Corinthian Christians are consistently called 'you' in distinction to 'we' / 'ourselves' / 'us', e.g. 3:1–3; 4:5). That plugs into the **Who am I? tool**: Moses is being compared to Paul and the apostles, not to us.

Who are we then? We're the beneficiaries of Paul's ministry, just as the Israelites were beneficiaries of the ministry of Moses. We're the ones who need a veil over our faces, the ones double-distanced from the glory of God . . . except . . . *through Christ the veil is taken away!!*

We need Paul to bring us the message of the new covenant that was entrusted to him and the other apostles. In this sense, he is the equivalent of Moses who relayed God's words to the people. But we don't need Paul as mediator. The 'we all' of verse 18 suggests that we join him in his front-row, dress-circle seat, as together we behold the glory of the Lord revealed in the gospel.

Figure 7

In the gospel of the Lord Jesus Christ we see, even more clearly than Moses heard, a revelation of a God who is merciful and gracious, slow to anger and abounding in steadfast love.

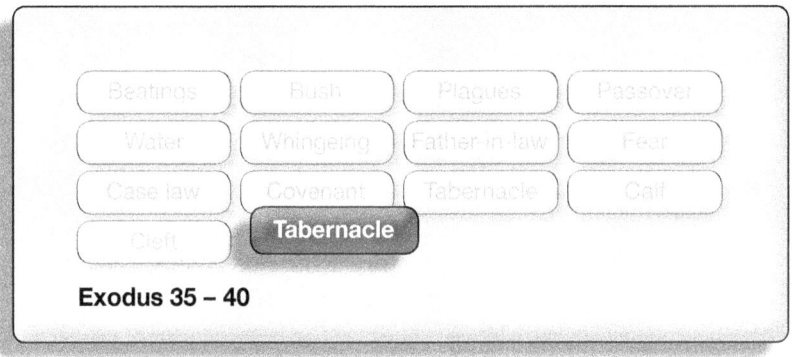

Exodus 35 – 40

What Exodus hasn't got in common with IKEA

As you enter Richard's living room, your eyes alight on a beautifully crafted dining table and chairs, together with a made-to-measure TV cabinet and a bookcase in matching oak. Richard's father-in-law makes furniture as a hobby.

Andrew, on the other hand, got all of his stuff from IKEA.

Some hours into assembling the JOKKMOKK™ table and chairs and no fewer than seven BILLY™ bookcases, Andrew turned up at the local tool-hire store, holding the ubiquitous Allen key between trembling fingers: 'Do you have any way of motorizing this?' It was all smiles on the way home, armed with a power drill fitted with a hexagonal drill bit. The smiles were short-lived. Did you know the planks in the box can be assembled to *look like* a JOKKMOKK™ chair in a number of different ways, but there is only one secret combination for which the final piece will fit? Even after the project is completed, you sit down for lunch somewhat gingerly, always wondering whether the screws left over were significant.

The final part of Exodus reads much more like a Richard's father-in-law project than a failed IKEA one. In chapters 25 – 31, the author recorded in great detail the *instructions* Moses was given for making the tabernacle. Now in chapters 35 – 40 he repeats the same details almost verbatim as he narrates the actual *construction* of the tabernacle. Using the **Context tool** to compare the construction with the instruction, you discover that things are done exactly right. Not a single screw left over.

All the different pieces of the tabernacle are mentioned again: the ark, the court, the golden lampstand, the acacia wood table, the bronze basin, the altar of incense, the priestly garments, and so on. Each item is described in the same terms: the materials used, the dimensions, the order in which it is made. Not one tanned ram's skin is missing: not one onyx stone, not one goat skin! Here's a flavour of how it goes:

> INSTRUCTION: 'You shall make a lampstand of pure gold. The lampstand shall be made of hammered work: its base, its stem, its cups, its calyxes, and its flowers shall be of one piece with it' (25:31).
>
> CONSTRUCTION: He also made the lampstand of pure gold. He made the lampstand of hammered work. Its base, its stem, its cups, its calyxes, and its flowers were of one piece with it (37:17).
>
> INSTRUCTION: 'And they shall make the ephod of gold, of blue and purple and scarlet yarns, and of fine twined linen, skilfully worked' (28:6).
>
> CONSTRUCTION: He made the ephod of gold, blue and purple and scarlet yarns, and fine twined linen (39:2).

INSTRUCTION: 'You shall make an altar on which to burn incense; you shall make it of acacia wood. A cubit shall be its length, and a cubit its breadth. It shall be square, and two cubits shall be its height. Its horns shall be of one piece with it' (30:1–2).

CONSTRUCTION: He made the altar of incense of acacia wood. Its length was a cubit, and its breadth was a cubit. It was square, and two cubits was its height. Its horns were of one piece with it (37:25).

And so on and so on, through each and every component part, down to the tiniest of details. 'But why?' you ask, **Author's Purpose tool** in hand, 'Why does the author go to so much trouble describing exactly *what* they made, when your readers already have such a detailed copy of the building plans?'

Remember, these are people who've just made a golden calf (to use the **Context tool** once again). Three times they promised that 'all that Yahweh has spoken we will do' (19:8; 24:7; cf. 24:3), but they didn't do it! Gold that was destined to make a temple lampstand was fashioned instead into a calf. But now, thanks to God's grace, they are obedient. The gold destined for a lampstand is fashioned into a lampstand. All that Yahweh had spoken they did, exactly according to instructions.

(It's true of course that their obedience doesn't last for ever, and for the rest of the Bible the cycle of sin abounding and grace much more abounding will continue. But there is an ultimate happy ending which this temporary happy ending foreshadows.)

Proof that everything really, really, really is back on track
So complete is the restoration of the relationship between Yahweh and the people, that it's as if the whole sorry business

with the calf had never happened. The **Structure tool** reveals this particularly vividly. Thanks to Barry Webb from Moore College, Sydney for setting it out for us so clearly:[1]

> A. The presence of God foreshadowed (25:1–9)
>   B. Instructions given for making the tabernacle (25:10 – 31:11)
>   C. The Sabbath (31:12–17)
>   D. The tablets of the law (31:18)
>   E. The golden calf (32:1 – 33:23)
>   D. The tablets of the law (34:1–35)
>   C. The Sabbath (35:1–3)
>   B. Instructions carried out: the tabernacle built (35:4 – 40:33)
> A. The presence of God realized (40:34–38)

This type of multilayered sandwich structure is often called a 'chiasm' and turns up fairly often in the Old Testament. Frequently, it is used to highlight the turning point in a narrative, where everything is reversed. For example, there's a chiasm in Genesis 2 – 3 that hinges around the Fall (Andrew is preaching on this at the moment): Adam is formed from dust (A) and given fruitful work (B) and a wife for whom he is thankful (C), and despite their nakedness they are not ashamed (D). When they disobey God's word and eat of the forbidden tree, everything is turned upside-down. They are naked and ashamed (D), Adam blames his wife (C), his work becomes painful toil (B) and he returns to the dust (A). There's another reversal-chiasm in 2 Kings 5. At the start, Namaan is leprous and Gehazi is clean. At the end, Namaan is clean and Gehazi is leprous. All is reversed. We could give many other examples.

The remarkable thing about the chiasm here in Exodus is that there is apparently *no reversal*. Nothing changes. That's the whole point.

Yahweh plans to dwell in the midst of a people he has brought out of the land of Egypt, out of the land of slavery. And *even though* they turned away from him in idolatry, he comes to dwell with them. Not in a halfway-house tabernacle some distance from the camp. Not in a scaled-down version with less gold, or IKEA-like craftsmanship. Plan A goes ahead unchanged. The relationship between Yahweh and the Israelites really, really, really is back on track.

The Exodus cloud survey
The book of Exodus ends under a cloud (40:34–38), but with none of the usual negative connotations of that phrase! We need to use the **Context tool** one last time to uncover the special significance of clouds in this book of the Bible.

1. As the people left Egypt, Yahweh went before them 'by day in a pillar of cloud' (13:21). This cloud-pillar protected them from Pharaoh's army (14:19–20), and 'Yahweh in the pillar of fire and of cloud . . . threw the Egyptian forces into a panic' (14:24).
2. When the Israelites whinged about having no bread, 'the glory of Yahweh appeared in the cloud' to promise them manna from heaven (16:10–12).
3. Yahweh told Moses that on Mount Sinai he would come 'in a thick cloud' (19:9). Sure enough, 'on the morning of the third day there were thunders and lightnings and a thick cloud on the mountain' (19:16).
4. When Moses went into the halfway-house tabernacle, 'the pillar of cloud would descend and stand at the entrance of the tent, and Yahweh would speak with Moses' (33:9).
5. When Moses was hidden in the cleft in the rock, 'Yahweh descended in the cloud' (34:5).

The cloud, then, signifies the presence of Yahweh. It is associated with his glory, his guidance, his protection, his fearsome power, his covenant and of course, his *name*.

Having completed our cloud survey, the stage is set for the final paragraph of the book. It is a breathtaking way to finish:

> Then the cloud covered the tent of meeting, and the glory of Yahweh filled the tabernacle. And Moses was not able to enter the tent of meeting because the cloud settled on it, and the glory of Yahweh filled the tabernacle. Throughout all their journeys, whenever the cloud was taken up from over the tabernacle, the people of Israel would set out. But if the cloud was not taken up, then they did not set out till the day that it was taken up. For the cloud of Yahweh was on the tabernacle by day, and fire was in it by night, in the sight of all the house of Israel throughout all their journeys.
>
> (40:34–38)

So What? tool

We've come a long way in a short time. We've learned God's name and we've seen him in action. His aim was that 'you will know that I am Yahweh' (6:7; 7:5, 17; 8:22; 10:2; 14:4, 18; 16:12; 29:46; 31:13). Now we know. So what?

- What have you seen of the character of Yahweh? How would you say you've got to know him better through the book of Exodus?

- What have you learned about yourself? Are there things of which you need to repent?

- What have you seen of the Lord Jesus whose shadow has been glimpsed so often?

> **BRAINBOX ASIDE: Exodus-inspired Psalms**
>
> We've asked you to meditate on some of what you've learned from Exodus. Some of the Psalms do the same, and their meditations on Exodus may help us to apply it more deeply.
>
> Have a look at Psalms 77, 78, 105, 106, 114 and 136, one at a time. Use the **Quotation/Allusion tool** to identify the various links to Exodus. (There are more than you will find on first reading.) Use the **Author's Purpose tool** to discern the particular lesson that each psalm wants to draw out. (They don't all use Exodus in the same way.) Use the **So What? tool** to ponder the implications for your own life situation.
>
> Happy digging!

Appendix 1:
Did the Exodus really happen?

Did the Exodus really happen? Some people would say no. But then they'd also say that Jesus can't have walked on water, can't have fed 5,000 people unless there was spare bread hidden in a cave, and can't have risen from the dead. Rising from the dead is impossible, they say. And so is parting the Red Sea.

Those people don't necessarily want to tear Exodus out of the Bible; they just want us to treat it like a story or a poem. They only become annoyed when you insist that these are actual historical events. But that means that they are going to end up being annoyed with Jesus and his apostles.

The parting of the Red Sea is mentioned as a historical fact in 1 Corinthians 10:1 and Hebrews 11:29. Stephen, the first Christian to be killed for his faith, obviously believed in the burning bush (Acts 7:30), as well as other 'wonders and signs in Egypt and at the Red Sea' (7:36). And Jesus really thought that God fed the Israelites in the desert with manna from heaven (John 6:32).

If you're a Christian, that will be enough for you. Having said that, it's worth tackling two of the big objections, namely, 'it's scientifically impossible' and 'it's archaeologically unproven.'

'It's scientifically impossible'

The argument goes like this: science proves that miracles are impossible, because they contradict the laws of nature. The Exodus account contains miracles. Therefore the Exodus didn't really happen. It sounds like a knock-out punch. But the logic isn't as watertight as it might first appear.

C. S. Lewis, the famous Oxford professor, explained to an atheist friend:

> 'Well, I think the laws of nature are really like two and two making four [said the friend]. The idea of their being altered is as absurd as the idea of altering the laws of arithmetic.'
>
> 'Half a moment,' said I. 'Suppose you put sixpence into a drawer today, and sixpence into the drawer tomorrow. Do the laws of arithmetic make it certain you will find a shilling's worth there the day after?'
>
> 'Of course,' said he, 'provided no one's been tampering with your drawer.'
>
> 'Ah, but that's the whole point,' said I. 'The laws of arithmetic can tell you what you'll find, with absolute certainty, provided that there's no interference.'[1]

Science observes consistency. It studies repeatable, observable events, and attempts to describe and explain them. You drop a banana from your bedroom window, and it accelerates towards the ground at 9.81 meters per second squared, give or take a bit for wind resistance. You drop a banana from the top of the London Eye (because you're a scientist and this is an important experiment, as you explain to all the puzzled tourists), and it accelerates at 9.81 metres per second squared. It's always the same for bananas dropped from different places on earth. It's a law of nature.

Laws of nature are based on what we observe. They tell us what is usually the case, what has been the case for every banana dropped so far in human history. But they cannot *prove* that there will never be an exceptional banana. There's nothing, in principle, to stop the God who chose 9.81 meters per second squared as the optimal acceleration of bananas one day adding a couple of zeros to the underlying gravitational constant and causing chaos in greengrocers the world over. There's nothing to stop him tampering with the drawer.

Sceptics are fond of quoting the Scottish philosopher David Hume (1711–1776) who argued against miracles in his *Enquiry Concerning Human Understanding*. But what they often don't realize is that, in this same essay, Hume attacks the principle of induction, one of the foundations of modern science. Inductive logic requires that the future be like the past; it assumes tomorrow's bananas will behave the same as yesterday's, and therefore that the laws of nature formulated yesterday will work for tomorrow. But Hume asks, 'How do you *know* this? Why should the future be like the past? What logical argument can you give to underpin this assumption?' The atheist has no answer.

Ironically, the Christian does have an answer. God likes order. He sustains his universe in a uniform and consistent way. That's why the principle of induction works. That's why you can get the same results from banana experiments conducted on different days of the week, in different laboratories around the world. That's why science is possible.

God is kind to greengrocers. He doesn't mess with the acceleration of bananas. It's not his habit to tweak the laws of nature just for fun. But (and here's the crucial point) there's nothing in science to tell you that he *couldn't* make an exception if he wanted to. And the whole point about miracles is that they are exceptions. They are one-offs. If quadriplegics regularly picked up their mats and walked home, how come the crowd in Capernaum had 'never [seen] anything like this'?! (Mark 2:12). If it were easy to walk on water at room temperature (we're not talking a frozen lake here), how come the disciples were 'terrified' when they saw Jesus do it (Mark 6:49–50)? If the Red Sea were in the habit of parting to allow safe passage, why did the Israelites think that they had been cornered by the Egyptians (Exodus 14:10)? They were just as surprised to see a miracle as we are to read of one.

What should a responsible scientist do with a miracle claim? She should investigate the evidence! And if there is evidence that the laws of nature are being broken, she should ask herself, 'What is the God who made the world and controls nature and who normally wouldn't allow something like this to happen trying to *tell* me?' The one thing she shouldn't do is reject the evidence because it doesn't fit with her faith in atheism. That would be very bad science.

Our top recommendation for those who want to take this further is 📖 *God's Undertaker: Has Science Buried God?* by John Lennox (Lion).

'It's archaeologically unproven'
The argument goes like this: there are no Egyptian records that specifically mention the Exodus, nor any archaeological remains to confirm that the Israelites were ever in Egypt in the first place. Therefore, the Exodus didn't really happen. It sounds like a knock-out punch. But the logic isn't as watertight as it might first appear.

All the events described in chapters 1 – 14 of Exodus took place in Egypt's East Delta, a fan of mud deposited over many years by the annual flooding of the Nile. If you wanted to build with stone, you had to transport it all the way from the south of the country. But one thing that wasn't in short supply was mud. And there was no shortage of slaves to make bricks out of it!

The trouble with things made out of mud, however, is that after a while they go back to being just mud, which isn't so good for archaeology. The few things built from stone didn't fare much better. Stone was so expensive that the cheapest way of building a new structure was to pull down an old one and recycle the stone. If you wanted a new cinema, you'd have to demolish the bingo hall first. And that means that archaeologists looking for bingo halls are going to be disappointed. In fact you'd be lucky to find the cinema, because quite a lot of the stone ended up sinking into the mud.

To sum up, hardly *anything* survives. Now, you're thinking, what about the Pyramids, they're still there? Yes, but the Pyramids are way down in the south, where the stone comes from. If the Israelites had set up camp next to the Sphinx, you could hope to find some preserved remains – you might even dig up an Israelite sandal. But if you're up north by the sea, you're going to be digging up mostly mud.

And what about the lack of Egyptian records? Put yourself into Pharaoh's shoes. You've just been humiliated by a bunch of foreign slaves, with the loss of a full chariot squadron. How much effort are you going to make to ensure that your defeat is remembered by future generations? You're hardly going to commission the construction of a new temple to commemorate it. In fact, if you can keep it out of the history books (which as a fascist mega-dictator with impressive powers of censorship, you probably can), then you will.

The other problem with Egyptian records, of course, is that 99% of them haven't survived because . . . yes, you've guessed it, they sank into the mud.

In summary, there are all kinds of reasons why we wouldn't expect archaeological evidence for the Exodus to be available today, over 3,000 years later. But to conclude that it never happened is like saying your friend never built a sandcastle because you couldn't find it on the beach a week later. That doesn't mean archaeology is useless. If anything, some of it rather impressively supports the biblical account. For the enthusiast, we'd recommend 📖 *On the Reliability of the Old Testament* by the influential archaeologist Kenneth Kitchen (Eerdmans). Here are just a few of the highlights:

- We know that the Egyptians regularly used slave labour for building projects. There is even a painting in the tomb of the vizier Rekhmire, dated circa 1450 BC, that depicts slaves making bricks in exactly the kind of conditions described in Exodus 1.
- Exodus 1:11 tells us that one of the store cities built by the Israelites was called Rameses. Archaeologists tell us that the Egyptian King Rameses II built a huge city and named it after himself. Taking account of the fact that Hebrew and Egyptian are written using different alphabets, the names are an exact match. The really cool thing, though, is that no-one making up the story of Exodus at a later date could possibly have got this name right. By 1070 BC Rameses had disappeared – all the stone was moved north and recycled to build another city called Tanis. Until recent archaeology recovered the name, no-one (except the writer of Exodus that is!) remembered that Rameses ever existed.
- In Exodus 13:17, God decided that the Israelites should not take a shortcut through Philistine country, because of the possibility of getting into a war. The war scenes of

Sethos I at the Karnak temple in Thebes depict a whole series of Egyptian fortifications that lined that route. Archaeologists have even excavated some of the military remains. No wonder Yahweh advised an alternative route.

Appendix 2:
Commentaries, copying and catastrophe!

Commentaries are very useful, but when copied they lead to catastrophe! In a moment we're going to recommend a few of our favourite Exodus commentaries. But before that, here are two important health warnings:

First, you should never blindly trust a commentary. The same goes for any Christian book you read or preacher you listen to or random article on 'Midwifery in Ancient Egypt' that Google throws up. You should imitate the Jews in Berea who are famous for 'examining the Scriptures . . . to see if these things were so' (Acts 17:11). Care is needed with even the most faithful commentary, and with a dodgy commentary, of which there are many, blind trust will lead you away from Jesus.

Secondly, you should never allow yourself to consult a commentary as an alternative to your own hard work on the text. The commentary gives you a structure, and so you don't bother wrestling with the structure for yourself. The commentary assumes that 'Moses is me', and you assume that he is, without questioning the validity of this interpretation. And so on. This way, we never develop our own skills in Bible reading and never see past our favourite teacher's blind spots. Because we're lazy by nature, someone else's quick solution will always be preferable to a couple of hours at the desk. We need to be on our guard against this. Beware of study Bibles in particular – the eye-movement needed to move from the tricky verse to someone else's 'solution' is so small that an iron will is needed to resist it!

If God had intended that we consult a modern Old Testament scholar as our final authority, then we would do well to remove Exodus from our Bibles and print the words of that scholar between Genesis and Leviticus instead! But as it is, God has chosen the book of Exodus itself as the means by which he will speak to us.

As a safeguard against commentary-copying catastrophe, we try to abide by two rules:

1. We never consult a commentary or a web page until we have done at least an hour of our own work without one. That means that, when we turn to what someone else thinks, we've already heard what God says. We're much more likely to spot a hobby-horse ('Is Exodus 15 *really* about the role of women as musicians in the ancient world?') or a glaring omission ('How come he makes nothing of God hardening Pharaoh's heart – is he ashamed of God's sovereignty?'). If you've become commentary-dependent, then the first hour is going to feel like cold turkey. You might even have to get someone to disable your laptop or lock your study Bible in the garage.
2. We never work from one commentary only. The temptation to follow blindly is too strong. *It's better to use no commentary at all than to use only one.* If you use two (more if you can afford them), then they are bound to disagree at some points and that makes copying impossible. You have to decide *which* to follow, and that means evaluating and weighing arguments by looking at the Bible for yourself. Commentaries used in this way

actually promote more, not less, toolkit use, and stimulate a closer reading of the inspired word.

Here are a few of the Exodus commentaries that we looked at:

- Brevard S. Childs in the Old Testament Library series (SCM Press, 1974) was one of the most significant scholarly publications of the last century. At a time when academics were speculating endlessly about half-verses and attributing different bits of the same paragraph to four or five different supposed authors, Childs urged them to look at each verse in its Exodus context and in the context of the Bible as a whole. Good job, mate! But Childs is not an evangelical, and his writing is technical, so this won't be the best place to start for most readers.
- John D. Currid in the EP Study Commentary series (Evangelical Press, 2000) offers a faithful commentary that gives helpful pointers towards application.
- John I. Durham in the Word Biblical Commentary series (Thomas Nelson, 1987) is full of exhaustive and exhausting detail and sometimes misses the wood for the trees.
- Peter Enns' NIV Application Commentary (Zondervan, 2000) is probably the one we found most useful. Credit to him for the 'seeing God – seeing the pavement' thing. We were a little cautious though about some of the 'Contemporary Significance' sections – too quick to assume that 'Moses is me'.
- Terence E. Fretheim in the Interpretation series (John Knox Press, 1991) is one of the most insightful – he was the one who gave us the breakthrough on Moses killing the Egyptian in Exodus 2. At other times, he is very disappointing, such as when he says that 'the death of the king in Egypt provides possibilities or opportunities for God that were not available heretofore' (p. 47).

It's beyond us how someone could read Exodus and get the impression that Yahweh waits his turn, impotent until events turn in his favour!

- Keil & Delitzsch's *Commentary on the Old Testament* (Hendrickson, 2006) is full of fascinating detail and shouldn't be overlooked just because it was written in the nineteenth century – new isn't always better when it comes to understanding the word of God.
- Alec Motyer in the Bible Speaks Today series (IVP, 2005) is clear, accessible and faithful.
- William H. C. Propp in the Anchor Bible series (Doubleday, 1999) is worthy of mention only as a warning. Like the false teachers described in 2 Peter, who 'do not tremble as they blaspheme the glorious ones', he writes in a snide and cleverer-than-thou tone that might be forgiven when reviewing a cheap novel, but not when dealing with God's holy word. Peter goes on to warn us that such teachers, 'blaspheming about matters of which they are ignorant, will also be destroyed in their destruction' (2:10–12). Pray for him to repent, and avoid his book. It's astonishingly expensive anyway.

Finally, we loved the collection of essays on Exodus presented at the Moore College School of Theology and now published as Brian S. Rosner and Paul R. W. Williamson (eds.), *Exploring Exodus: Literary, Theological and Contemporary Approaches* (Apollos, 2008). And we are big fans of Tremper Longman III, *How to Read Exodus* (IVP Academic, 2009). And we can't recommend highly enough L. Michael Morales, Exodus Old and New: A Biblical Theology of Redemption (IVP Academic, 2020). Both highly recommended.

Appendix 3:
The Bible toolkit

Here is a quick recap of the tools introduced in *Dig Deeper: Tools to Unearth the Bible's Treasure* (IVP, 2005).

Author's Purpose tool
The biggest question we can ever ask of a passage in the Bible is simply, 'Why did the author write this?'

Bible Timeline tool
Where is this passage on the Bible timeline? Where am I on the Bible timeline? How do I read this in the light of what has happened in between (e.g. the other side of Jesus)?

Context tool
Words come within sentences, sentences in paragraphs, paragraphs in chapters, chapters in sections . . . A text without a context is a con!

Copycat tool
Is the author holding up one of his characters as someone we should imitate or whose likeness we should avoid?

Genre tool
There are many genres in the Bible – e.g. song, historical narrative, genealogy, law. Identifying the genre is important to how we interpret a passage.

Linking Words tool
Whenever you see a 'therefore' ask what it's there for! And the same goes for words like 'because', 'so that', 'for' etc.

Narrator's Comment tool
Sometimes the author breaks into his narrative to explain what's going on (a kind of 'Pssst, reader, make sure you understand this . . . ').

Parallels tool
Bible poetry doesn't tend to rhyme. Instead, it says the same thing twice in different words (and so you get two chances at understanding it): 'Twinkle, twinkle little star; Shiny, shiny, tiny nebular'.

Quotation/Allusion tool
When the author quotes or alludes to another part of the Bible, we should turn there to see what ideas he is picking up on.

Repetition tool
Sometimes the author says something more than once to make sure we don't miss it. Sometimes the author says something more than once to make sure we don't miss it.

'So What?' tool
What implications does this have for me? For my church? For an unbeliever?

Structure tool
How has the author broken down his material into sections? How do these sections fit together?

The 'Who am I?' tool
Whose shoes in the passage are we supposed to step into? If any!

Tone and Feel tool
Pay attention to how the point is being made. Is it happy? Tragic? Comforting? Frightening? How does the author want you to feel about what he is saying?

Translations tool
Read the passage in more than one translation, just in case there is a nuance one version has missed.

Vocabulary tool
Bible words have Bible meanings. Be alert in case the author is using a familiar word in an unusual way.

Notes

Beatings
1. John M. Frame, *The Doctrine of the Christian Life: A Theology of Lordship* (P. & R. Publishing, 2008).
2. There are other ancient accounts of babies hidden in baskets, notably the myth of Sargon of Agade. Some have assumed that the writer of Exodus has merely adapted an existing fairy tale for his own ends. However, it is quite likely that the Sargon myth *postdates* the biblical account (although it purports to narrate the life of Sargon the Great c. 2334–2279 BC, it was written much later, perhaps during the eighth century BC). See further Tremper Longman III, *How to Read Exodus* (Downers Grove: IVP Academic, 2009), pp. 54–56.
3. Don Cormack, *Killing Fields, Living Fields* (Monarch, 2001).

Plagues
1. The word 'harden' in the ESV translates three different Hebrew words. But there doesn't seem to be any consistent difference in the way that they are used.

Water
1. From the Christmas carol, 'O Come, O come Emmanuel' (author unknown).

Whingeing

1. In the original *Dig Deeper* we explored these same passages using the **Bible Timeline tool**. Sometimes more than one tool will get you to the same answer.

Fear

1. Rob Lacey, *The Street Bible* (Grand Rapids: Zondervan, 2003), p. 53.
2. C. S. Lewis, *The Lion, the Witch and the Wardrobe* (London: Collins, 2001), p. 89.

Case law

1. Source: 'UK chooses "most ludicrous laws"' (BBC News Website: 7 November 2007).
2. Strictly speaking, the case laws only run from 21:1 – 22:20. The surrounding material does not conform to the genre of case laws, but consists rather of instructions or moral imperatives. Thanks to Desi Alexander for this clarification.
3. Similar laws concerning ox-goring can be found in other ancient Mesopotamian law codes, for example the Code of Eshunna and the Code of Hammurabi. This need not trouble us, for as Tremper Longman III points out, 'The uniqueness of biblical law is not based on the fact that its ethic and formulation cannot be found elsewhere' (*How to Read Exodus*, p. 62). God's common grace extends beyond the bounds of Israel, so that even pagans have a moral sense that murder is wrong (for example) and that ox-goring is bang out of order!
4. See www.angelfire.com/pro/lewiscs/humanitarian.html
5. Reading Matthew 5:38–42 using the **Quotation/Allusion tool**, we might at first assume that Jesus is overturning this principle. That seems unlikely, however, in the light of Matthew 5:17 (**Context tool**!). Almost certainly Jesus is speaking out against the *misuse* of the eye-for-eye principle to justify personal vendettas, something

that Exodus itself sought to guard against: 'he shall pay *as the judges* determine.'
6. The Christian Institute provides a range of helpful resources (www.christian.org.uk).

Tabernacle (1)
1. If you create your own diagram from the ESV text, you'll find that 'Holy' comes out a bit smaller. That's because we based ours on the Hebrew word *qadosh*, so that it counted the 'sanctified' and 'consecrated' words together.
2. Further correspondences are identified by G. K. Beale, *The Temple and the Church's Mission: A Biblical Theology of the Dwelling Place of God* (Leicester: Apollos, 2004), pp. 66–80.

Calf
1. G. K. Beale, *We Become What We Worship: A Biblical Theology of Idolatry* (Nottingham: Apollos, 2008), pp. 77–78.

Cleft
1. The idea of the Israelites having some, albeit mediated, access to God's 'face' is also present in 33:14, which literally reads 'My *face* will go with you, and I will give you rest.' Unfortunately this lies beyond the reach of the **Translations tool** because we couldn't find an English version that renders it literally. You would have needed the **Learn Hebrew at Bible College tool**.

Tabernacle (2)
1. Barry Webb, 'Heaven on Earth: the Significance of the Tabernacle in its Literary and Theological Context', in Brian S. Rosner and Paul R. Williamson (eds.), *Exploring Exodus: Literary, Theological and Contemporary Approaches* (Nottingham: Apollos, 2008), p. 156.

Appendix 1

1. C. S. Lewis, 'Religion and Science' in *God in the Dock: Essays on Theology* (London: Fount Paperbacks, 1971), pp. 47–48.

related titles from Inter-Varsity Press

Dig Deeper
Tools to unearth the Bible's treasure

Nigel Beynon & Andrew Sach

'A great work on knowing God better, learning his will for your life and reading your Bible'
- Mark Dever

Listening to God speak to us through the Bible is like picking up a telephone and hearing your Creator at the other end of the line. It should be exciting, life-changing even. But sometimes it seems more like a long-distance call, with static on the line, and it's hard to make out what our Father is saying. Maybe our own interpretation is such guesswork that we're in danger of putting words into God's mouth.

The passionate aim of this book is that it should help you to 'correctly handle the word of truth' (2 Timothy 2:15) so that you will experience God's clear guidance in your life, come to know him better and grow to love him more. Your Bible reading will never be the same again.

'Just brilliant. Practical and accessible, and will revolutionize the way you read the Bible.' - Linda Marshall

ISBN: 9781844744312 | 192 page paperback | RRP: £8.99

Available from your local Christian bookshop or via our website at **www.ivpbooks.com**

DIG DEEPER
Bible Toolkit

CHECK OUT THE WWW.DIGDEEPER.TOOLS WEBSITE FOR VARIOUS FREE RESOURCES

including quirky videos introducing some of the tools (e.g. the one where Andrew makes seven costume changes in seven seconds) and a series of ready-to-go small-group Bible studies on 1 & 2 Kings that you could use in conjunction with this book.

FIND OUT MORE

www.ingramcontent.com/pod-product-compliance
Lightning Source LLC
Chambersburg PA
CBHW070145100426
42743CB00013B/2823